# The Rise of
# Establishment Politics:
## Essays On U.S. Politics
## During the Bush and Obama
## Adminstrations

# TORRANCE
# STEPHENS

# Other books by Torrance Stephens

a matter of attention – novel
last from go - novella
fast and gamin' – short stories
butter brown – short stories
rock star, stud, gigolo – short stories
freak type scene – short stories
dirt behind my ears – essays
brilliant dumb – essays
nobel neocolonialism: u.s. west asian, north and
east african foreign policy under the obama administration - essays
the legacy of the bush-obama keynesian dialect
and income inequality in america: a journal
negro comfortable – essays
for u who left me while I slept – poetry
late nite winds of club paradise – poetry
anonymous guest – poetry
why I'm a gangster - plays

RAW DOG BUFFALO PRESS
PALMETTO/MEMPHIS/WHEREVER
© 2016 BY
TORRANCE STEPHENS
@RAWDAWGBUFFALO

"You cannot adopt politics as a profession and remain honest."
**Ambrose Bierce**

"Politics is not the art of the possible. It consists in choosing between the disastrous and the unpalatable."
**John Kenneth Galbraith**

"Politics is the gentle art of getting votes from the poor and campaign funds from the rich, by promising to protect each from the other."
**Oscar Ameringer**

"If voting made any difference they wouldn't let us do it."
**Mark Twain**

# The Rise of Establishment Politics:
## Essays On U.S. Politics During the Bush and Obama Adminstrations

TORRANCE STEPHENS

# Introduction

First, I write for myself. I enjoy it and as opposed to talk with other people **Ad nauseam.** My preference is to contain my thoughts in complete form, or as complete as possible and pen them to paper. Moreover I write like I talk. Many of the essays herein were from either newspapers or other publications I have written and/or served as a contributing writer for or my blog. Still others, just thoughts I recorded on yellow legal pads.

Any case, since the second term of the Clinton Administration, and more so even during the middle of the George W. Bush administration until the start of the Barack Obama administration, the policy making of decades past were in front of my very eyes, morphing into some new protoplasmic political mutant. Suddenly, it was difficult to determine political policy making between republicans and democrats. In fact the blur between Clinton, Bush and Obama was so supersaturated that if they did not openly affiliate with any political party, on paper their policies would be completely similar if not the same.

As opposed to having distinct political variances, through the common denominator of capitalism and American exceptionalism, the citizenry started to take a back seat to a select and privilege ruling elite that resulted in a singular monopolistic political modus operandi.

Instead of American being the manufacturing center of the world, a huge part of our economy became supported on war, the things we make for wars and a financial service sector that fed on profiteering from fractional reserve banking and collateralized debt; all of which were supported on the backs and labor and service of a growing lower and shrinking middle class America.

1

However, as the average American started to pay attention, and notice the rhetoric of both major political policies was actually the same, and that the policies implemented continued to enrich them and their contributors from large corporations, K Street and Wall Street, a new colloquialism began to be accepted to describe these observations – "the Establishment" and "Establishment politics."

The establishment, regardless of political affiliation, is more into name-calling, blaming and pointing fingers while giving thirty second sound bites on corporate owned cable news stations than solving or even trying to solve problems.  Given this lack of ability and imbued ineptness and superficial nimble problem solving, it became easier to fan the flames of identity politics and artificial reforms to hide their authentic inability to address any other cause not involving their self-enrichment, consequently to the disgruntlement of the electorate.

The average voter considers the establishment as the party elites and wealthy who have more to gain from dividing and breaking the U.S. populous into groups and factions, in an effort to disguise their true intention to maintain control, than servicing the need, desire and will of the people. The establishment is not blue-collar and has never had roots in the working class poor, and frequently speaks as they are concerned with the middle class but never mentioning the poor.  So in simple terms, when the citizen speaks of the "establishment," we are referring to the people whom were directly responsible and in many ways the cause, of the economic doldrums our nation is facing.  When we speak of the "establishment," we are talking about the folks, hidden and tucked away neatly inside the beltway and sometimes in New York whom raised tuition to where it is unaffordable, foreclosed on our homes, raised the prices of our rent and groceries, poisoned our drinking water and sent us off to fight wars and return in body bags so that they can sell tanks to some despot in the Middle East that can cut them a check. This is the establishment and these essays are an attempt on one author's behalf to express and document the tangible uselessness and criminality that describe to a tea not only their mental disposition but also their professional comportment. **Torrance T. Stephens**

# 1 - Friday, January 26, 2007

*"There are some who, uh, feel like that, you know, the conditions are such that they can attack us there. My answer is: Bring 'em on. We got the force necessary to deal with the security situation.* "- George W. Bush, July 2, 2003.

Bush Baby, can you just stop for a moment to realize that the U.S. will never be observed as an objective and honest party in Iraq. Is it impossible for you to learn from history? This is not the first time that a Western nation has attempted to install a government under the guise of imperialism in Iraq. History shows us that the British were there for more than two decades and they had to eventually cut and run – just as we will.

We (US government) claimed we would bring an American democracy to the people of Iraq. We claimed such even though we knew the people of Iraq did not want or ask for an American style government. Now we see that it may take more than we have at our mental prowess to deal with the Iraq quandary. It is apparent that the current administration does not have any conception of solving this problem. How does sending an additional 21,000 troops to Baghdad deal with the root issue at hand and better yet, how did the President come up with such a number as being enough when former General Powell suggested you needed at least 500,000 to do the job correctly?

We cannot count on the ruling government we have established there to do the job. In all actuality, Prime Minister Nuri al-Maliki is no different from Saddam Hussein; after all, we built up Saddam like we have posted up Al-Maliki. The only difference is that the plan that he offers his people in the form of a democratically centralized government is not the plan of his nor the Iraqi people, but rather a US developed initiative. The current administration seems to miss the big picture. Money and troops will not lead us to a solution or a reduction of animosity towards the west, in particular the

United States. We can see this from what we have failed to do in Afghanistan since we invaded the country in 2001 (the White House has requested an additional $8 billion from Congress for the war in Afghanistan).

Through all of this, we just get more dead folks. So far, 53 US troops have been killed in Iraq this month, many of which are in central Baghdad. Nothing is improving in Iraq and just this morning, a bomb killed 15 people and wounded 55 others in Baghdad's Friday morning pet market. Yesterday, a bomb killed at least 34 people in Baghdad and all of this while US military is heavily engaged with insurgents.

President Bush will be remembered for several things in the history books: 1) pre-emptive military action, 2) his US-led invasion of Afghanistan in 2001 and 3) Iraq in March 2003 and maybe even a military conflict with Iran before the end of the year. So do not be so quick to think these problems will go away with the addition of 21,000 more troops and a constitution in Iraq because we will be talking about and seeing this war and the others on television for at least the next decade, if not even more.

## 2 - Friday, February 23, 2007

President Bush has signed an $82 billion military spending bill that was overwhelmingly supported by the House of Representatives that will, assist to create electronically readable, federally approved ID cards for Americans (the Real ID Act). The concept, which is stated to be the brainchild of Wisconsin Rep. Sensenbrenner, is outlined primarily as an anti-immigration measure. It would require state drivers' licenses and other such documents to meet federal ID standards established by the Department of Homeland Security. It is supposed to help immigration because in theory it will prohibit states from issuing driver's licenses to illegal aliens (as if illegal aliens won't drive if they do not have licenses – laughable politics as usual).

In three years from now all U. S. citizens and anyone in the country will need a federally approved ID card to travel on an airplane, open a bank account, and make use of any government service. One form of information contained on the card is "common machine-readable technology" that Homeland Security will decide upon. It will also have "physical security features designed to prevent counterfeiting, or any other fraudulent activity." I take this to imply that biometric information such as retinal scans, fingerprints, DNA data and radio frequency identification (RFID) tracking will be on the card. It seems to be a waste of money on several levels. First passports already have/contain radio frequency identification chips embedded in them. Then there are estimates that it may cost $120 million dollars that could actually (God forbid) be employed for real security.

My concern is that the legislation REAL ID will pass because it was attached to legislation that funds military action in Iraq, which means that it basically was accepted and pushed on the people without hearings or debate anywhere. To add salt to the wound, reports have suggested that production of the card and associated data will be outsourced to a private corporation. Reports also suggest that DHS head Michael Chertoff personally ordered this option to be chosen, which in essence outsourced State and Constitutional rights from state DMVs to a private corporation. All that is accomplished is that the federal government supersedes states powers and states' systems for issuing driver's licenses.

Then there is the uncanny question in my mind as to why I have not read or heard anything about REAL ID in the newspapers or on television anywhere? Where is the open discussion on the side of liberty? All this does is help to establish an Orwellian Police State since in October 2004 the Intelligence Reform and Terrorism Prevention Act became law and established and put in place new security measures for driver's licenses as recommended by the 9/11 Commission Report. Welcome to the inevitable, a National ID is coming and honestly, none of this is required nor does it increase homeland security or illegal immigration. As such, this is a tort of intrusion I cannot live with.

### 3 - Saturday, March 17, 2007

Call me Candide (Voltaire is my favorite writer), but I was kind of anticipating a warm recognition for an anniversary last week. No, not the Biggy ten years after his death anniversary, nor the 25-year anniversary of *The Message* (Grand Master Flash and the Furious Five) although such is worthy in these eyes. And most definitely I am not speaking of the 25 year anniversary of John Belushi's death. I was just expecting that the 50th anniversary celebrating Ghana's independence from Britain would have gained some recognition from African Americans over in this camp. I mean we have problems to solve but the first step in solidarity is the recognition of respect for mutual self-determination. Ghana was the first sub-Saharan country to break with its colonial power.

Even the U.S., I mean President Bush, sent a delegation to honor this momentous occasion. The Presidential Delegation to Accra, Ghana for the 50th Anniversary of Independence was led by Alphonso Jackson, Secretary of Housing and Urban Development, and included Pamela E. Bridgewater, United States Ambassador to the Republic of Ghana, John J. Danilovich, CEO, Millennium Challenge Corporation, Ronald A. Tschetter, Director of the Peace Corps, Jendayi Elizabeth Frazer, Assistant Secretary of State (African Affairs) and R. Timothy Ziemer, Rear Admiral, United States Navy (Retired), Coordinator for the President's Malaria Initiative. Leave it to President Bush to be disrespectful and send second tier dignitaries to this historic event. As well, I can comprehend the sentiments of former President Jerry Rawlings, who criticized the event.

Sure, everybody knows that on 5 March 1957, Britain formally transferred power to independence leader Kwame Nkrumah. Nkrumah was a great and powerful man and still is relevant today if you asked me. Not to mention, he wrote one of my favorite books ever by African thinker, *Africa Must Unite*, inclusive of *The Mind of Africa* by Peter Abrahams. *Africa Must Unite* was the first book that explained racism in terms of power (page 15). Kwame Nkrumah guided Ghana to independence on March 6 1957 and was the first black nation to achieve such in Africa. In particular given that Ghana was once the world's top exporter of cocoa and a leading producer of gold.

I was just optimistic that there were fans of self-determination and history as I am myself. Guess the song we shall overcome will always be enigmatic for us as a collective. Or maybe, just maybe I don't look at enough television and think too much.

### 4 - Monday, July 30, 2007

I love the news, but not for the purposes of being educated and informed objectively about what is going on. However, in this zest for information, I am often reminded that there is a substantial corpus of information that is weeded out by a small group of zealots that tends to rub me the wrong way. Case in point is the war on terror and the purposeful focus on Iraq and Afghanistan. Although these are mentioned, it is really not known about the third front in this effort, the war the US is conducting in Somalia.

Since it has been known that Al-Qaeda has been operating in Somalia, the Kenyan, Ethiopian, the United States in concert with the Transitional Federal Government of Somalia have been fighting the Union of Islamic Courts and the joint forces since December 2006.

Historically, Somalia wars were between factions and warlords. However now, there is a discernable difference between the parties involved in the fighting. The main participant is the U.S. military, which has been providing financial support to the fighters such to become an organized resistance groups against bands of Islamic fundamentalists in central and southern parts of Somalia.

To date, the current administration (White House and State Department included) do not confirm that they are supposedly at war with Al-Qaeda groups in Somalia. A recent Newsweek report confirmed that "gunship attacks as well as AC-130 aerial assaults" occur "on a daily basis" and that the U.S. Military has "deployed American commandos to hunt down remnants of Islamic hard-liners, both from the carrier USS Dwight D. Eisenhower offshore, and across the land border from Kenya in the south."

The Bush administration is aware of all of this; however, we citizens of the U.S, as a whole are not. This should not be unexpected since the Bush administration has launched operations all across the Muslim world. Now, it is in Africa and against the Union of Islamic Courts, which controls the majority of southern Somalia.

So what does this say? Number one, read newspapers from outside of the US if you desire accurate information of our actions worldwide. It also shows us how as a nation, we have started a war between Ethiopia and Somalia (two of world's poorest countries) in an effort to fight terror which will likely result in the destabilizing of two African countries. Nothing good can come of this for Africa or the US, but that does not seem to matter, because if this war continues, it will likely incur serious harm to U.S. interests in Africa – another fine mess you have gotten us into.

## 5 - Thursday, August 02, 2007

Sometimes I wonder whom side they on - government and politrixters. It seems that it is not on the side of logic, the public's hard work, or the community. The priority has to be elsewhere. After the collapsing of that bridge in Minneapolis, Minnesota it dawned on me that the general infrastructure of this country, with the exception of a few cities like Atlanta, do not regularly work on highways, add runways, or replace water lines in the city.

Most cities I travel too in the states, including my home town of Memphis have poor highway systems and such makes me think that the rest of the infrastructure needs serious examination too. From Flint, to Orlando, to DC even, the highways systems, if any indication of other systems is on the surface dilapidated and antiquated.

In Minnesota for example, two reports published since talked about "the bridge's deck truss system" having "many poor fatigue details on the main truss and the floor truss system" but that is beside the point. The point is that we as Americans, especially the political class are more focused on the present and quick fixes and are no far thinking anymore as; let us say Africans, East Indians and the Chinese. We fail to think long term and lean towards "if it aint broke, don't fix it" instead of "let's make some new main."

Then there was before this, the c, which was lauded as an "engineering marvel". Which opened 13 January 2006 at a staggering cost of $14.6 billion? Noted problems of this edifice included thousands of leaks in the ceiling and wall fissures and a fatal accident on July 11, 2006 where part of the ceiling collapsed connecting I-90 to the Ted Williams Tunnel.

The problem outside of the aforementioned could be that these things are controlled by quasi-governmental agencies of "Authorities" or "Systems' "that are not accountable

11

to the general public. Like the Massachusetts Turnpike Authority.

Even still, we will see a lot more problems; it was only a matter of time given that 2005 was the 50th anniversary of the creation of the U.S. Interstate Highway System. So that means it's old as fuck, and just imagine the dams and yes, the bridges. But hat can one expect, when the folk yell vote for and place in office prefer to build shit in Iraq that are blown up after we finish, not even talk about such as a campaign issue, or worse with folks from Katrina still with nothing two years later. Glad I know America is a republic and not a democracy and landowners make decision. Boy am I thankful for my 11-acres. Maybe something good can come of this, maybe; vast improvements to infrastructure, Prince starting a scholarship fund for the children of victims - showing these new artist what civil responsibility is (not making it rain in a strip club).

### 6 - Thursday, August 30, 2007

Believe it or not, having no government in Iraq at the moment means more problems for the folks we consider our allies, Especially Pakistan. Pakistan, a country that is run by a man that took over in a military Coup and still prefers to wear his military uniform as opposed to a suit and tie. What's the problem you say? Well let me put it like this.

In a speech to the European Parliament foreign affairs committee last year, Pakistan's President General Pervez Musharraf blamed the United States and the West for "breeding terrorism in his country by bringing in thousands of mujahedeen to fight the Soviet Union in Afghanistan and then leaving Pakistan alone a decade later to face the armed warriors," according to an article in the Pakistan's Daily Times published last year.

Now these same forces, once friends to the US are our enemies and we put them in place. The situation is pre-

12

carious for Musharraf since they are trying to push him out of leadership the Malcolm X way – by any means possible

You would expect this given that Bush and the General are all buddy buddy now, all would be god in the home front for the General – but it is not. Although I really don't think the General wants such to be the case, Bush has fallen hook, line and sinker for his partner in crime. For one, being in Bed with Bush is not god from his perspective. Although he says he is partner in fighting against Bin Laden, truth is al-Qaeda had found a safe haven in Pakistan and that his country is slowly becoming more assumed with radical Islamic fundamentalist that he may need to keep is military closer than the norm.

Then taking money from The US will place his grip on the People of Pakistan in a more tenuous sight. Bush administration has offered $750m over the next five years in aid for the tribal agencies, including $300m to help to patrol the Pakistan-Afghanistan border. Sop to make a long story short, it may not be too long before we get a news bulletin saying the general has fled in exile or has been killed and Bin Laden and his folks have their hands on real weapons of Mass destruction. Talk about creating your own reality.

### 7 - Thursday, September 13, 2007

One could argue that since we declared war, invaded and subsequently occupied Iraq that things have been getting better (that is if you are a recovering cocaine addict as is our current head of state). Otherwise, such an assertion would be fatuous. Ever since major military operations ended in Iraq some four years ago, we have still been conducting major military operations. Not to mention, inconsistent and running water, electricity and high unemployment was unheard of prior to our invasion and is now a daily reality for some 70 to 80 percent of the Iraqi populous.

Add to that the fact that the government we installed is basically dissolved, with leading figures such as Judge Radhi al-Radhi, who ran the Public Integrity Commission set up by Paul Bremer recently resigned due to death threats (a fortune for him since a substantial number of politicians we have installed have already been killed).

We were told that the troop surge was supposed to reduce the insurgency and create an environment for a democratic government to function. Instead, it has gotten worse, with almost 4000 troops to date losing their lives, another 20,000 wounded and now there are recent reports of a cholera epidemic in the North of the country that is heading down stream. All of this, 7 years after 911.

The President and his assorted collection of puppets still say we are making progress. Which indicates to me that his only strategy for the country is to leave office and have the mess there for another administration or more to clean up?

This if such is the case, it means that his plan has only fostered Sunni extremism, an environment ripe for sectarian and civil conflict and more than 1000 attacks on US forces weekly. Truth is we destroyed Iraq and do not even care nor count the number of Iraqi civilians that have been killed or wounded. Yep, we are making progress – progress toward being the most hated country in the entire Arab world.

### 8 - Wednesday, September 19, 2007

Growing up I was a big fan of comic books. I loved the super heroes and arch villains even more. I didn't lean much for DC comics and the likes of Superman and Flash, but towards the Marvel group with Luke Cage, Black Panther, Iron Man and the Avengers. Although I haven't picked one up in a while, I do see a new Super Hero or super villain arising on the world stage – China.

14

The way I see it, China is about to move in front of all these rinky dink powers of the G-8 great west delegation. And they doing so with professional criminal without a criminal record accuracy. You can start off with the Yuan. It was devalued for the first time in a decade in 2005 when the changed it from being valued on the dollar to a group of currencies.

Since then, the Yuan has appreciated 6.35 percent against the US dollar and this past July hit a new high against the US dollar given a trade surplus at mid-year projected to be US$100 billion. But that's not all. If that wasn't enough, they started attacking our kids via toys. Most of the recently recalled toys (lead or choking hazards) were made in China (about 75% of U.S. toys are now made in China). And these re dangerous toys after the Chinese get through:" Easy-Bake Ovens that trap children's fingers in openings, resulting in burns; Portable baby swings that entrap youngsters".

Then there is the toothpaste that has been reported to contain diethylene glycol, a toxic chemical used in engine coolants that has been distributed through the US to hotel chains. Add to this, the recall of some 450,000 tires made by Hangzhou Zhongce of China due to a fault that increases their chances of blowing out while driving causing the driver to lose control.

I tell you, we worried about the Middle East when China is on a slow creep to jump over us. It shouldn't be long, seeing that the trade surplus grows larger each day between US and China, which was estimated at 15 billion with US in august 2006, and their exports increasing yearly. I guess this means a new super hero or super villain is on the block so find some kryptonite.

### 9 - Sunday, October 21, 2007

From what I can recant of US Presidential politics, most mother fuckas wait till they get out of office before they are commemorated. This is to say they don't commemorate themselves. George W. Bush, I guess aint the average run of the mill mother fucka. I guess he couldn't wait until he was out of office, or better yet, dead, to have his memorial constructed. My folk (who a navy seal) say that all you can see is cranes all over the place in Baghdad and that security there is even thicker than the green zone. What are they building? Supposedly the new U.S. Embassy, but since when has an embassy been constructed on a 104 acre site? I have seen Embassy's all around the world, in particular U.S. Embassies. From Nigeria to Ethiopia, to Benin to Zimbabwe and places in between, none have ever been that large. Some have reported that it is even larger than the United Nations site in NYC and the a third smaller than the National Mall in DC.

Located beside the Tigris River, the embassy will have features the Iraqi people used to have - a defense force and uninterrupted electricity and water. With 21 buildings, it will be ironically located down the street from Saddam Hussein's former presidential palace.

All I was able to find on the new embassy was the articles I have hyper-linked here. It is so secret that I concluded it has to be more than an embassy, but rather a presidential library for Mr. Bush. After all, what more fitting a location than Iraq? We gone be up in that camp for years to come if the exercise historically recorded by the British is any indication. This embassy is a strong indication of this, being the largest in the world.

To me doing such tells the Iraqi people and government who is really in charge and who has the final say on their democratic government. But why would the Iraqi's be mad? Although they say the U.S. ambassador to Iraq will believing in a house approximately 16,000 square feet, it seems like he trying to build his library in a place where he will be most renowned. Picture that, Bush Presidential Library of

16

Bagdad. It is the least he can do since he assisted in the destruction of the historical libraries in the country. I'm just glad it's over there.

## 10 - Monday, November 05, 2007

Politrix, the art of hustling and shysternomics personified. Take the Honorable Mr. John Murtha. Other than his recent concerns for bringing troops home from the war effort in Iraq, what stands out in my mind about Jones here is the FBI sting video he made in 1980 in which he told a man supposedly who was a lawyer for a rich Arab looking for a Visa that the way to do business with him was to invest in his district. Although he was hesitant to take the 50 stacks in cash from the agent, he in essence said he did business this way (via pay offs) all the time.

Reading a Wall Street Journal last week, I found out a little more about Mr. Murtha. It said that he had funneled hundreds of millions to his district over the years, establishing a defense-based economy for his district. Even in the current 2008 House defense spending bill, they say more than 40 earmarks worth approximately $166 million is slated to go to corporations that have established businesses in his district.

The problem is that these businesses are getting loot for work (if you can call it that) that doesn't add any productive value other than government waste. Take Concurrent Technologies. They have gotten, through Murtha's effort, more than 200 million in defense contracts for what the WSJ described as "vaguely worded research." Examples include $2 million for "Advanced Combatant Materials Research" and the "Electronic Commerce Resource Center", a non-profit military program funded by Murtha designed to help small businesses use Internet technology. Basically the received millions to provide Internet access to these businesses when such services and access was already available.

17

Murtha also help establish the Johnstown National Drug Intelligence Center in 1994. Since its start, it has received b his efforts more than 500 million dollars. Operating as an extension of the Justice Department, the US General Accounting Office reported that it was a waste because it duplicated on-going efforts conducted in Washington and around the country. Then there is MTS technologies, a company that was started by a man who used to shine shoes at Murtha's Minute Carwash in Johnstown.

These are just a few of the problems with Congress the way I see tings. I guess it is ok to be responsible and to get jobs for one's district. I just don't think it is the right thing to do at my expense as a tax payer, in particular when the money is being wasted. I'm certain he is not the only one. I wonder how much we could have benefited as a country if it was applied to education, both at the primary and college level. Or for health care? Maybe I'm just a hopeless romantic, maybe they would have made more companies like the ones above, to waste the money and pad their pockets. Whatever the case, that Murtha F**ka is a straight up crook.

## 11 - Wednesday, November 14, 2007

They say there are no other folk like kinfolk. In this period of a presidential transition, it is difficult for me to see at best and frustrating at worse, that there lies the possibility that the same family will have its last name plastered in the White house again Bush-Clinton, or Clinton-Bush. For some sordid and clandestine reason I feel that these two families are related, that they are maybe fourth or fifth cousins, with the same friends, the same political support and same economic interest. Not to mention the disposed megalomania that both branches of this family tree possess.

I don't know about others, but as far as I can remember, since the elder Bush days, either a Bush or a Clinton has been in the hollow halls of that fat crib on Pennsylvania Avenue. I mean, since 1989 our illustrious leader has had either Bush or Clinton as their Surname. If Hillary wins, well you make the call. That just so happens I am not too comfortable with this as some other may be. Sure folks want Bush out of office, but what is the difference between a Bush and a Clinton – the same political machine politics are in existences, it is just that they pay political dues to different organizations.

I wish I had a stellar record as a political pundit – but I do not. Otherwise this Libertarian here would sign up to run thangs up in this camp. But I know personally, I would "a-fear" most of my competition and most of the voting public. Nah, I'm a landowner and got more clout than any singular voting serf.

But I just had to say it. I had to get it off my chest. Aren't you tired of the same ole same ole? If not try to make this man understand, what is a difference between a Clinton and a Bush, outside of political Affiliation? Add to hat how can you vote for Hillary? Cause folk here just do not get it.

### 12 - Friday, November 16, 2007

Got damn revenuers. I tell you, at this rate, I will never run out of stuff to say about our government. I just found out that my tax dollars have gone to file an indictment against the all-time home run leader Barry Bonds. A federal grand filed this for perjury and the obstruction of justice lying.

Of all folks, the Federal government have some nerve to call anybody a liar or to accuse anybody of obstructing justice. Last I heard, the filibuster was still used in the hallowed halls of congress. And why, for steroids? From what I have read, this is the result of a four year investigation. Four years – they don't even take four years to investigate each other (senators and congress persons), or to investigate the fowl-up of FEMA with regards to Katrina, or why the mortgage lending industry has led to an increase in foreclosures across the country, or why it take 93 cents to make one Canadian dollar, or why the Veterans Hospitals of American can't provide health care to men and women who serve our country.

Steroids are a marvel of science. They are used every day. In medicine alone, they are prescribed daily to people who do not play sports to assist them with recovering after surgery. Steroids are also extremely useful (both male and female sex steroids) in mediating or protecting against cardiovascular disease (CVD) and hypertension in some individuals. Anabolic-androgenic steroids are even used for alcoholic liver disease. Why can't sports figures use them but regular folk like you and me can?

And why Barry Bonds, they didn't indict Rush Limbaugh for his drug addict behavior of abusing Oxycontin. Shit, I bet half the folks in the legislative, executive and judicial branches of government are taking some prescription medication that is a steroid by the definitions of organic chemistry that learned back at Morehouse. Organic chemistry is the study of the properties of carbon-based compounds that are organic.

Just tell me, who are the members of this Grand Jury and why not make them take drug test to discern if they using steroids. Why aren't their names made public? We know that our current President is a recovering alcoholic and cocaine addict but they don't indict him, and he running the country, spending more money than we have and sending men and women to die daily in a war over an emotion.

I tell you, is it just me, or is there no pragmatism in government anymore? I'm a libertarian, but I feel that George Orwell when he penned 1984 and Aldous Huxley when he wrote *Brave New World* may have been right. You think Ray Bradbury will be next, I man will they start burning books like they did in *Fahrenheit 451*? Or is this a replication of an old David Letterman skit called "Stupid Pet Tricks?"

## 13 - Monday, December 03, 2007

In a few years from now, I may not be able or worse, imprisoned or executed for writing some of the things or expressing my personal views, I the manner I desire on such topics. In particular if Senate Bill S.1959 has its way. S. 1959 a bill to establish the National Commission on the Prevention of Violent Radicalization and Homegrown Terrorism, and for other purposes. The billed has just passed in the house (H.R. 1955) and now is headed to the Senate. To add another stupid pet trick to the mix, the bill only targets United States citizens and make continuous use of basic Constitutional protections it targets in an effort to fight supposedly home grown terrorism.

The general purview for such a law is scary for two reason, first it is buttressed on the assumption that since 9/11, America is less safe (been the same to me all my as a man of color). The second is that the wording is unclear and vague at best. Based on the way it reads, this act could be easily used to label anyone or group that has strong criticism of the government. For example, in section 899a, "violent radicalization" is stated to "means the process of adopting or promoting an extremist belief system for the purpose of facilitating ideologically based violence to advance political, religious, or social change." In the same section, ideologically based violence" is defined as "the use, planned use, or threatened use of force or violence by a group or individual to promote the group or individual's political, religious, or social beliefs. Now I may be wrong, but are they saying "thought crimes" in the Orwellian sense, or as they put it, "Planned use" can be looked as an act of terror? Would my thoughts if perceived as hostile to a selected administration and being against our war efforts, posted on the Internet via my blog be considered as acts of terror?

I say yes. In section 899b, finding (3), it is written that "The Internet has aided in facilitating violent radicalization, ideologically based violence, and the homegrown terrorism process in the United States by providing access to broad and constant streams of terrorist-related propaganda to United States citizens."

The bill is supposed to be an amendment to the Homeland Security Act of 2002 and in the house, was sponsored by Rep. Jane Harmon (D-CA) -in picture. If you asked me, she should be the poster girl for what a homegrown terrorist looks like. For anyone who attempts to restrict my personal liberties under the guise of fear and paranoia, is the real terrorist – so stand up lil momma.

## 14 - Sunday, December 16, 2007

Jones main, it's on. The news has not even made it yet but it appears as if the fragile whatever you call it we put up in Iraq to represent a government has officially dissolved. You see, while most of us up in this camp were sleeping last night, the Turks were sending warplanes over into Iraq to bomb the Kurds. I suspect they were targeting a political group called the Kurdistan Workers Party (PKK). The Turks have outlawed the group, but it seems kind of feculent to outlaw an organization in another country, which operates basically autonomously. The say these raid were some 60 miles into Iraq. Meanwhile on the otherwise of the field (it is football season), all I read about Afghanistan' from this side of the block, is that we are winning the battle, that more and more Taliban fighters are being killed and that each day we work with or favorite Dictator in Pakistan to make progress in terror (that is if progress includes more videos circulating in Pakistan that show 12 year olds beheading a Pakistani's accused of being U.S. spies). The Taliban is always executing and beheading folks who they claim to be spies for the US, we just never see it on TV unless the spies are actual US citizens. I mean Bush and the US media obviously think that it take four such acts or more to equal one US life. But at the same time, Afghanistan's President Hamid Karzai is asking for more help to develop his armed forces.

Well I guess the Bush administration has some good news to report by their standards, after all the aforementioned and said dictator, just lifted the emergence rule he just placed over his country because they would not vote for him (during a period in which HE amended the country's constitution). At least we can be thankful that George W. Bush isn't a general, no telling what he would have done by now.

### 15 - Monday, December 24, 2007

For me, I think 2007, has been the year of the premonition. But before I go farther. I want to thank all yawls with the birthday wishes and those who purchased books. And I can't forget my tiger's pimp slapping Roy Hibbert and Georgetown. To both of the aforementioned, I am still smiling.

But back to premotating, I have premonated (don't know if either are words but I don't really care) that these folks, in particular the politicians, may be hitting the pipe too much – for they will say anything to get a vote. Such was even my premise in stupid pet tricks.

Check this: Mitt Romney is a perfect example, and while telling some people a tall tale, he got cold busted. Gone say some shit like he remembers seeing his father as a child, marching alongside with Martin Luther King Jr. (I'm trying not to laugh at that shit now). The problem is that it never happened and was completely fabricated. He even said it was just a figure of speech, a metaphor. He was just pretending – make believe.

The Republican presidential said this while making a speech on faith and politics earlier this month in Texas. To quote him, Romney said: "I saw my father march with Martin Luther King."

They say it was the biggest speech of his political career thus far. Titled speaking on "Faith in America" at College Station, Texas.

Jones even started to like the sound of that shit and this past Sunday while on NBC's "Meet the Press." He said,

"You can see what I believed and what my family believed by looking at our lives. My dad marched with Martin Luther King." He probably would have kept on saying this if it had not been for some serious investigative reporting by the Detroit Free Press and The Boston Phoenix. Not to mention the eyewitness accounts of one veteran Michigan civil rights activist who told the DFP that George Romney never marched with Dr. King.

Trying to cover his ass, Romney's campaign cited a 1967 book written by Stephen Hess and Washington Post political columnist David Broder. They even released a press statement saying in essence; yes Virginia there is a Santa Klaus. King ain't even march in Grosse Pointe in 1963 because he was not even there. Not To mention records indicate he was out of the country in some school in Europe at the time he say he saw or heard such.

But what it tells me is that not only is he a liar, but he don't even know his father that well and aint spend that much time with him if he got to lie for them both. But they got the loot and time to investigate steroids in baseball, but neither of the priors to put themselves in check.

### 16 - Thursday, December 27, 2007

I just wanted to thank the laws for putting into place a new crime to come – Eyeball stealing. Sure there is no code for it, or no fancy name like homicide, it too shall come to pass. Trying to get what they can out of biometrics, the FBI wants to use precise body measurements unique to every human being, to help them fight crime. The new FBI plan announced last week notes that the agency plans to spend a $1 billion dollar on the effort. Now these fools cannot even solve or prevent identity theft and its text-based information so whom will they be able to secure a massive database of biometric data? I mean it last forever. One could even be dead and the still could be committing crimes with your eyeball. The only good may be a new specialty in plastic surgery or ophthalmology in changing and replacing human iris and retinas. According to the Washington Post, the FBI is going to give somebody a 10-year contract that would contain information on all from iris patterns, scars and the way people walk. The way I see it it's my information and the FBI doesn't own nor have the right to steal and keep my information – I am not no coin, stamp or baseball card. Add to that I have a major question concerning who will get this massive no-bid contract.

They call it "Next Generation Identification" According to Thomas Bush III, assistant director of the Criminal Justice Information Services section (I think he is related to the President but I can't find any info on him nor can I prove it yet). With this type of technology, it may be possible to scan a person with a video camera in a public place and capture and collect imagoes of their face and iris without their knowledge and/or permission. This is worrisome; I mean it was just a few weeks ago I was complaining about the amendments to the homeland security legislation and now this.

There is also limited information and research on the future utility of Biometric database security and full range of potential. At the West Virginia University Center for Identification Technology Research, which is less than an hour from the FBI's biometric facility in Clarksburg, researcher is already underway dealing with clandestine iris image capturing from 15 feet to 200 yards. In Germany, scientist conducted the only large scalp study I could find on the subject. Conducted from October 2006 through January at a train station in Mainz, Germany, findings noted the ability to match correctly 60% of study volunteers in the daytime but less than 20 percent at night. All I am saying is who is down with helping me develop optic image refractive contacts, it may make us millionaires in no time.

### 17 - Friday, January 04, 2008

It was my intention to not discuss the caucus results of Iowa and or Barack Obama at all so early in the election. I was hoping after reading a substantial corpus of blogs from around the globe I would see a majority of the implications discussed. Especially after such a "stunning" victory (others words not mine; stunning to me is 50% of the votes).

For the record, your boy here likes to stack a little change. Easy change which means using your brain. Maybe some consulting or statistical data analysis mostly, but also in them markets, precious metals and Forex exchanges. I mean I bought my first stocks when the DOW was at 3500 (which fell today 266.84 to 12,998.28). So one could suffice to say I have accrued and nice sum of chump change.

However, I feel that whoever the next President is, there will be something to deal with that won't be easily dealt with either with the rhetoric of experience or new leadership. This week, an ominous and unfortunate event occurred, the price of oil went over the mythical $100.00 a barrel mark. Although it returned below that level, it did happen.

True, the price is a function of increasing demand, especially from countries in Asia like china and India, but it is also a major consequence of the falling dollar. It is also a function of disruptions abroad due to civil unrest and war. Not to mention, that in America, there is no productivity in manufacturing, we make nothing anymore, no job creation and as noted in 2007, a 40% increase in consumers filing of bankruptcies. The latter itself is the function of another indicator - the increase in foreclosures and the decline of the housing market.

Now I'm no economist, but I think I was taught well by my 10th grade Econ teacher at Hamilton High School in Memphis, Dr. Moyer, but I can say that when Bush came in, we had a surplus and now, by the next 120 day, who knows, maybe inflation. And the Federal Reserve may not be able to do nothing about it. I mean as long as I have been investing, in particular in forex and precious metals, the dollar normally increased proportionally to the price of Gold. Now the dollar goes down as gold (and oil) increases. This scares the fuck out of me and the 300K plus I have saved over the years.

So yes, Obama won Iowa. I do wish him the best albeit I am supporting neither democratic or the republican nominee. Nonetheless, still more states and regardless of whoever wins, I feel sorry for poor Mr. or Mrs. President, whoever they maybe.

### 18 - Sunday, January 06, 2008

Go figure, but seems to me before the Mitchell Report came out, each and every day, somewhere in the United States someone was talking about Barry Bonds, his use of steroids, and their often fatuous purview (since use of HGH is not illegal in baseball) and how they think he should have some ridiculous reminder behind his homerun record. Many of these folks are in many cases likely afflicted with respect to laying sport proficiently in the first place. And like magic, all of this talk stopped. Mainly because the folks who were talking made such sweeping statements that they have to eat crap with respect to who they think worthy to be in the hall-of-fame. Many said Barry, because of this would never make it.

The Mitchell Report named some of the golden boys: Rick Ankeil, Eric Gagne, Chuck Knoblauch, Andy Pettitte and Roger Clemons.

While being interviewed on 60 Minutes by Mike Wallace, Roger Clemens said he was never injected with illegal performance-enhancing drugs by his former trainer Brian McNamee, who told former senator George Mitchell he injected Clemens with steroids in 1998 and with steroids and human growth hormone in 2000 and 2001. Mitchell released his report on illegal performance-enhancing drugs in baseball last month. I looked at the show and saw him basically trying to save face. I aint gonna say he lying, but.....

Now maybe I am stupid, but if it takes a physician to prescribe lidocaine, why didn't a doctor do the injections? Moreover, he never mentioned that he had received any injections from his trainer in any of his previous denials regarding steroid use. Not to mention he was not a Biology major while at the University of Texas.

Since the Report, nobody talking about or picking on Barry Anymore. Add to that, now the same folks who said that he should not be in the hall of fame or that his record is tainted, will have to say the same about the names I called out earlier and that makes me happy. Unfortunately, since such is the case, they do not even discuss Steroid use in baseball and the assorted implications much anymore. No Barry, no steroids unless like 60 minutes. They didn't eve run a show on the topic until the golden boy himself was called out. Last week I was using allegory and my understanding of Moliere's *Tartuffe* to explain hypocrisy. This is another prime example. I mean it's like the governors in the world of sports talk have given the aforementioned, and Mr. Bonds by default clemency, a pardon, a commutation of sentence, or a reprieve.

So I think the moral of the story is it is ok to throw stones at glass houses unless the house got members of your family inside. Meaning if Roger gets in, so must Barry both with and without an asterisk.

28

## 19 - Tuesday, January 08, 2008

You know all good, and even great things come to an end. Such is also true for nation-states. The Roman Empire fell because it was fearful of technology, it had no more folk to conquer and because the Empire's economy could no longer be fueled by the exploitation of new colonies. They had to raise higher and higher taxes to maintain itself and its armies and the people pulled a Hall & Oates (can't go for that, no can do).

Babylon's fall came as a result the loss of commercial relationships with other nations and depopulation, although Biblical pundits use *Isaiah 47* and *Revelations 16* to assert that the fall was a punishment from God due to their "false religious system". And we all recant the fall of Constantinople by the he Ottoman Turks Empire in 1453. Today class, I would like to postulate that the next major empire to fall will be the United States of America.

From all I can tell, it should not be a strange observation that the country I am citizen of is going under. Some may suggest that what I am saying may be seditious, but I would just assert that my view is just that, an observation. And If I can tell, I'm certain folks involved in the machinery of government know also. I mean based on the way our economy functions alone, it got to break down one day.

There was even a report in the mid-1970s by the Stanford Research Institute and compiled by the SRI Center for the Study of Social Policy. To sum it all up, the breakdown will be that of our form of capitalism and democracy mainly as a function of globalism and monopoly capitalism. We talking about the greed and avarice that so many cooperate and political namesakes maintain where the people at the top always implement policy for their pockets as opposed to the betterment of the greater population – meaning they have a penchant for manipulating such to maximize profits for the individuals associated with these multi-national corporations.

And thinking about it, it is not that I am the first to say such. W. Cleon Skousen's book *The Naked Capitalist* talks about such as well as the noted Georgetown historian Carroll Quigley in his book *Tragedy and Hope*. I first heard of him when President Clinton gave him props during his inaugural address. The book is a historical work covering the period in the US between 1890-1960 (classic must read on REAL U.S. Modern history).

It examines the mechanics of international bankers and of the organizations they formed to influence behind-the-scenes political and diplomatic activity. He provides insight on groups such as the Royal Institute of International Affairs and the Council on Foreign Relations. I would suggest the 1300 plus pages to any lover of history. So revealing and detailed, that it was pulled from bookshelves and its publication was halted for several decades. He spoke of what he called financial capitalism and explained this tersely in his examples regarding the power of bankers, especially investment bankers over governments.

Just going over the copy I have recently brought all of the current thoughts to fruition, especially the decline in the US economy and the increasing impact that our government policies is having on the entire world. But it would not surprise me none if what I have described happens within the next decade or two. And this is on the real, based on my own objectivity, cross my heart and hope to die.

### 20 - Friday, January 11, 2008

With all this election stuff, it had almost slipped my mind that we were still at war in Iraq and Afghanistan and trying to contrive 5 speed boats as an act of war with Iran. Then there is the northern end of Iraq, where the Turks and Kurds going at it. But as expected they say things are going well when to me they are not.

If I was an Iraqi and running the government of Iraq, I would move to take our state back and urge all, Sunni's and Shite to join in battle with the Kurds against Turkey. This may engender nationalism of my people for Iraq, and at the same time anger the US, who move for a unified Iraq but really don't want one – and did I add, would likely be forced to help Turkey if such popped off. But this won't occur for we have effectively divided the country and encouraged secularism in the country with our pre-emptive policies and morosely laconic foreign policy.

We are now, since the surge (whatever that is) recruiting villagers of Iraq that are members of armed Sunni groups known as Awakening Councils. In theory they supposed protect their neighborhoods with the help of the US military. Haven't we been down that path before? In 2005 The U.S. military command in Baghdad acknowledged that they paid Iraqi newspapers to carry positive news about U.S. efforts in Iraq and we saw what that got us.

Now paying folks that want to see us dead and we know they want to see us dead like that's gone solve the problem and make the country whole and safe. The Awakening Councils are estimated to be 70,000-strong and growing. Such short sightedness tells me that the US has not even thought of the long-term implications of empowering folks that hate and want us out of their country and who also have sever disdain for the Shiite-led government established by the US. I mean these folks are very well trained and well-armed. Which begs to ask what will they do when we eventually withdraw troops (cause they will leave one day – just like the British).

Not to mention in November of last year, audits revealed that some 17K of these folks were being paid but not standing post. But what can one expect when u hire folks 10,000 at a time and pay $10.00 a day (quarter billion dollars a year).

31

But as I said and back to the main point, the country is divided and I am not the leader of the government nor Iraqi. The Kurds up north, the Sunnis and the Shite down below. We are funding the well-armed folks in the Sunnis who hate us and let a mainly shite government set up in the country. So we funding to rival militaries and expect that we leave, the country will be all peachy keen.

### 21 - Tuesday, February 05, 2008

Man, your folk here has lost complete respect for Lou Dobbs tonight. I used to listen to him and his drive towards dealing with illegal immigration in America. But tonight, folks got his panties pulled up his booty crack and got defensive.

I mean Janet Murguia put it down. She is the current La Raza President and CEO. I mean she made me see that Lou did not ever, really distinguish from Illegal and legal immigrants, He even tried to refute FBI and department of justice statistics showing an increase in hate crimes against immigrants, Hispanics, Latinos.

What upset me was when he made it into an attack on him, when the entire time she said Networks, all networks, not CNN alone. It was as if he was upset when she documented Dobbs paraded on television, people that belonged to white supremacy groups. I figure if they did, they did. Then he tried to say that since she could only go back to 2006, that it was not important, when he himself use info over the years (with immigration and the Iraq war) to buttress his positions.

She said Glen Beck, Pat Buchanan and others did the same. That he had used the individuals 18 times on TV and CNN 48 times for having folks own who parody hate speech. I don't think. He tried to make it an issue of the 2007 Comprehensive Immigration Bill (S.1348). Dobbs was so caught on his high horse, that he ignored the issue. Hers was hate speech. All slim wanted to talk about was hate speech, and how he and his network put representatives of hate speech, on at primetime and that we should hold networks accountable for putting them on the air. And what made me mad, was that he considered the Southern Poverty Law Center as unreputable when I know they have documented more lynching's and hate groups than the FBI. That lost a big point from me, since I am sure he would be the least likely person to be dragged from a car that I can think of.

But that was cool, I mean I seen dogs running with the tails between their legs. But during the next segment, that bitch nigga (Lou Dobbs) had the nerve to query, is that where we have come to in politics, pandering to individuals groups as opposed to the populous? I mean, I am a member of the NRA, but I hope he don't think we represent the America Collective. Dang, I mean he study media, he should at least know as a politrixter, you can't talk to Jews and African Americans and high school college students at the same time. I mean, what history has he studied, it has always been about white identity politics. The never cared before, and I'm still waiting to see u Dobbs or CNN or FOX, or MSNBC ask a white candidate about carrying the white vote. Mr. Dobbs, I just want to say, America is like any restaurant we go to, and thank goodness they ask us, what dressing we want before they just dump anything on our salad. Dang Lou, you sounded like Billy boy from FOX.

### 22 - Saturday, February 09, 2008
I know in my heart that I worry about the sons and daughters and husbands and wives of those engaged in military combat. And I sincerely will never wish for such an experience for my son or daughter for I believe it is like Michelle Obama said, that they are the only ones really making a sacrifice for our country. I just wish that the government and military appreciated and understood such.

My work in prisons and with the homeless shows me too much. That for example, I get tiered and hurt at the same time that at least a third that I have come across were veterans of Dessert Storm and of recent wars. In fact it turns my stomach. But I try not to show it working with them. I wished that, and believed that my government is me, and that it would make all the considerations possible to make the return of these individuals admirable. Unfortunately, it appears, as under the surface this is not the case.

I have just come to find out that the Army Surgeon General Eric B. Schoomaker doesn't have firm control of his administration. A few weeks ago, NPR ran a story reporting on a memo that advocated that the Army had told the Veterans Affairs Department not to assist soldiers with completing paper work that would challenge their disability ratings. Such paperwork can decide if a veteran will receive annual disability payments and health care after they're discharged from active duty.

Initially Schoomaker denied the allegations but later recanted saying that at the time he did not have nor saw the memorandum. It just amazes me how the top dog of all Army medical affairs had no knowledge of the aforementioned. Either he is inept or ha a bum staff or worse, doesn't read the material that comes cross his desk.

The memo was dated March 31 and concerned the meeting held the day prior on March 30 at Fort Drum Army base in upstate New York. Last year around this time, Lt. Gen. Kevin C. Kiley, Army Surgeon General and Commanding General of Army Medical Command, Lt. Gen. Kevin C. Kiley, was forced to resign over similar concerns regarding providing services to veterans.

Some have suggested that the issue is completely economic, pointing to the notion that the more the Army has to shell out for veteran disability, the less money they have in their budget for other activities - humbug. In fact the current situation in trying to reduce benefits for Veterans started back when Caspar Weinberger served as Secretary of Defense. A March 25, 1985, memo from the DOD office of general counsel, provided the Defense health officials the legal ground to "restrain military disability ratings without a change in law."

Now I know that with the multiple battlefronts we have opened around the globe that it is hard to deal with the number of soldiers wounded in the wars in Iraq and Afghanistan. In addition, as a health professional, I know that the people under the big brass are competent, and only have in their heart to provide the best service possible for them and are working assiduously to do such. I just think it is ridiculous that the administration cannot meet the level of their zeal at servicing. Not having enough wheel chairs for example is not their fault, but that of those in command, for they should also know that such in itself for example is a violation of the Americans with Disabilities Act.

I know my voice is limited, but I would like to say for the record, that treating anyone who serves in our military like an envelope without a stamp is foul. As if they (the DOD) just use up folks, and return them to sender as if their address is unknown. I figure if we have the resources to fight several wars, then we should, up front, have the resources available to take care of veterans when they return, without question. Moreover, the resources in leadership to make sure this happens.

If this could be implemented, the we wouldn't have folks coming back not getting the help they require; folks like Louis Bressler, Kenneth Eastridge, and Bruce Bastien, who are charged with the murder of a fellow soldier, Army Spc. Kevin Shields - who had served two tours of duty in Iraq. Bressler, the trigger man, was reported to have been discharged for medical reasons with Post Traumatic Stress Syndrome. But that's another story. All I am saying is that it don't (I'm country) make no sense to live in a country where inmates get better medical treatment than our service personnel. This is America, no matter what your status is, we should get the best medical care, especially veterans.

### 23 - Friday, February 15, 2008

Now back to our regular scheduled programming. I had a homeboy that used to play defensive back with the Washington Redskins and Eagles. When he finished playing football in college, right before the draft, he came home. At one of my infamous parties, we exchanged dap and talked. He spoke about the interviews he had with several NFL teams prior to the draft. He said he told them all "if you pay me enough, I will run into Brick wall." Now my Boy Barry hit hard, was Memphis Buck, and fast – all 6'2", 220 pounds of him. He led the NFL in interceptions as a rookie and had 2 interceptions during the Skins Super Bowl win over Denver when Doug Williams was the MVP. I say this as a metaphor regarding the future as it may come to fruition in November.

Most of you all know that Dr. Ron Paul was my first choice for the Presidency, followed closely by Senator Obama. But since it seemed as if folks didn't ascribe to my position, I'm going with Obama in the title game. However, many folks are so caught up on the primaries and his nemeses that we seem to be missing the bigger picture. A few weeks ago I asked why Black folk seem to vote hook, line and sinker for the democrats. Now, I feel that if things don't go as most expect, there may be a form of whiplash from African American voters.

The cynicism will rise extremely quickly if the democratic primary allows for the race between HilBill and Barack Obama to be decided by a bunch of elites Super delegates. As it stands now, with this inclusive of what has happened with the democratic primaries in Florida and Michigan, shit may really hit the fan. I mean, it wouldn't surprise me if all this sit ends up in court. Not to mention that the three co-chairs of the DNC Credentials Committee: Alexis Herman,

36

James Roosevelt, Jr. and Aliseo Roques-Arroyo, all served in the Clinton Administration. I just wonder how serving and working for her husband for 8 years may influence how they cast their super delegate votes.

On the other side of the aisle, Obama is already talking about November – a November where he most likely will be in the title game against John McCain. Although both democratic candidates say they are the best to face McCain, the truth is Obama has the best chance. Hillary says she can, but it would be easy for her to get beat down if she did face him in the general election. First, there are zillions in the GOP who hate her husband and her as well. Most folks would use the Clinton's as a rallying cry to motivate a stagnant party, even if many conservatives feel that McCain isn't conservative enough for them. Add to the fire that pundits like Rush Limbaugh recently said he would help raise money for Senator Hillary Clinton in order to unify the GOP.

Obama to me would be a stiff challenge for the GOP although some, like the ultra-conservative New York Post, owned by Rupert Murdoch's News Corps. Empire endorsed Obama in the New York primary, feel that it will be easier to defeat him. Why, well it brings us back to the feeling that hard liners hope that the race card, and the assumption that many still would not select an African American to be the President of the United States, as their player card.

Truth is he will be a visible difference versus McCain. First he will represent a strong generational difference, which McCain cannot challenge. Second, he will be a strong contradiction to McCain stance on the war in comparison to Clinton, who voted to support the war effort. Not to mention McCain sees us being in Iraq for another 100 years. So what's next? Well Hillary is already sending her daughter around to meet with the younger super delegates. For example, she recently had breakfast with Jason Rae who is a super delegate since he is a member of the Democratic National Committee from Wisconsin.

But the aforementioned is not the issue, it is the super delegates, who will the side with and what them three big wig Democratic Credential Committee folks will do. This has been a break out years for the democrats. It seems that they have been able to motivate young voters as well as pick up independent voters who have historically voted republican. However, if Obama has a slim lead nationally, but ends up losing via the super delegates, it may end up back firing on them. Especially among African American and young voters, who may be so disappointed, that the party that says it stands for unity may lose a major segment of its membership. Its ok for my boy Barry to say he will run into a brick wall if they pay him enough, but I don't think the democrats can survive running into a brick wall that may turn folks off from the voting and election process.

### 24 - Saturday, February 16, 2008

To the honorable Mr. Henry Waxman and Tom Davis: Why in the fuck are you wasting my tax money to hold Reform Committee hearings of Human Growth Hormone? I mean, it's nice for me to perceive that you are concerned, but forgive me if I find it hard to fathom that you actually care. I would like to say you both do have top-shelf tie game, but you are no doubt wasting my money.

Honorable Mr. Waxman, forgive me, but I prefer to get my information on science from scientist, of which I consider myself to be, and academic and scientific journals, of which I am certain you don't read, from the manner in which you stumbled over words and concepts you orated during the segment of CSPAN called Health Effects of Human Growth Hormones.

Of all folks Mr. Waxman, you need to consider HGH given your age, but that is another story. For some reason or

38

another, I feel that the time and money (of which your salary is paid) would be better spent on dealing with education or the issue of the homeless or prison. I mean, more folks are actually affected by the aforementioned than those that inject or consume HGH. Not to mention, your concern for B12 injections appears on the surface to be disingenuous and more prone for a discussion of fans of Roger Clemens.

As I looked at the lot of you listening to the scientific experts, I could not help but feel that they were talking over your heads, and that you all actually felt like sleeping. I say this for you all offered the penumbra that you were the kind of folks who slept through science class. I bet if I gave you a test on what the experts presented, you all would fail (without it being open book, or open note, or a take home).

If I were a gambling man, I would extend the prior assertion to spelling (albeit I can't talk) and or grammar, for I am willing to bet that you do not know what PERNICIOUS means. In either case, I would most likely have to give yawl a makeup test to pass.

So Honorable gentleman, please spend my money on important stuff, and don't even think about giving yourself a raise because you did this shit - conducted a study session on HGH.

Thank you sir, and I would like to reserve the remainder of my remarks, but I would like to add, that it is B-12, and not B-15 Mr. Waxman (u keep saying B-15 sir). B-15 is Pangamic acid and used for folks with high cholesterol, it is also an Ice Berg as well as a form of Military aircraft. I'm sure you have been in the House long enough to may have signed funding for it.

I thank you for your time and the chance to testify before your committee.

## 25 - Sunday, February 17, 2008

I guess Hillary Clinton used the 5 million she loaned her campaign a few weeks ago well. Seems that reports have come out now that suggest Barak Obama did not get a single vote in some 80 voting districts throughout the state of New York. Not a single one.

These districts included Harlem of all places. According to an article in Saturday's New York Times Metro Section headlined: "Unofficial Tallies in City Understated Obama Vote." A segment of the article read:

"Black voters are heavily represented in the 94th Election District in Harlem's 70th Assembly District. Yet according to the unofficial results from the New York Democratic primary last week, not a single vote in the district was cast for Senator Barack Obama.

That anomaly was not unique. In fact, a review by The New York Times of the unofficial results reported on primary night found about 80 election districts among the city's 6,106 where Mr. Obama supposedly did not receive even one vote, including cases where he ran a respectable race in a nearby district.

City election officials this week said that their formal review of the results, which will not be completed for weeks, had confirmed some major discrepancies between the vote totals reported publicly -- and unofficially -- on primary night and the actual tally on hundreds of voting machines across the city.:

The Times adds this relevant information: "The 94th Election District in Harlem, for instance, sits within the Congressional district represented by Charles B. Rangel, an original supporter of Mrs. Clinton."

I just wonder who she paid from her campaign coffers. Not saying she a cheat, but if they do it in baseball, or the New England Patriots do it, why not her? I mean, where she get her HGH from?

Well it would have been easy for me to talk about Wisconsin and Hawaii, and or to pontificate on the first week of March with the Upcoming Texas and Ohio primaries. Just as unde-manding, would have been to talk about John McCain's di-rect comments toward Barak Obama, or how Obama, is now pulling more voters from women, from whites and from the non-college educated folks that Hillary Clinton, which once upon a time ago was suggested to me, was her base.

Instead I am going to take another stab at revising history. It is well documented historically that Abraham Lincoln had seven debates across the state of Illinois in 1858. In fact the historical record has labeled these the "Lincoln-Douglas Debates."

The debates were between Abraham Lincoln and Ste-phen A. Douglas. They were battling for one of Illinois' two United States Senate seats. History also tells us that Lincoln lost these debates since he lost the election.

Douglas, a Democrat, was the incumbent Senator was a strong advocate of Popular Sovereignty, and was responsi-ble for the Kansas-Nebraska Act of 1854. Popular sovereign-ty suggested that settlers of federal territorial lands could de-cide the status under which they would join the Union – ei-ther free or slave.

Strange thing was that although he lost the Senate race to Douglas, he beat the same man for the 1860 race for the US Presidency. Although these debates framed the issue and difficulty of having a productive union in which some states were slave states, and others were Free states, the real debate from my purview was not with the Senator from Illi-nois, but from another Douglass – Frederick Douglass.

Frederick Douglass was probably the biggest critic of President Lincoln. It was he who got Lincoln to practice what he preaches to move beyond his rhetoric on morality and freedom. Although most would think that these two men were on the same page politically and ideological, they were not. Lincoln believed the primary directive of the North was to preserve the Union and not to end slavery. Douglass was the first to suggest and urge Lincoln to use of black troops to fight the Confederacy. He positioned that by establishing colored regiments in the Union army. Douglass wrote " every slave who escapes from the Rebel States is a loss to the Rebellion and a gain to the Loyal Cause I need not stop to argue…The negro is the stomach of the rebellion." He urged President Lincoln to urge equal pay for black soldiers.

Lincoln even said on the record that "If I could save the Union, without freeing the slaves, I would do it. If I could do it by freeing some and leaving others alone, I would do that. What I do about slavery and the colored race, I do because I believe it would help to save the Union."

Truth be told, the policy of the Lincoln administration was one of pro-slavery. Douglass unlike Lincoln, incessantly focused on the face of the war and stated "the mission of the war was the liberation of the slaves as well as the salvation of the Union. I reproached the North that they fought with one hand, while they might fight more effectively with two; that they fought with the soft white hand, while they kept the black iron hand chained and helpless behind them; that they fought the effect, while they protected the cause; and said that the Union cause would never prosper until the war assumed an anti-slavery attitude and the Negro was enlisted on the side of the Union."

Douglass was instrumental in getting Lincoln to see that the civil war was a struggle between freedom and slavery. For Lincoln was troubled by the view in the North that it was seen as a war for abolition of slavery singularly. This upset Douglass and in his meetings and dialogue with Lincoln made sure he understood that could have never been designed, with its talk of forming "a more perfect union, establish justice, insure domestic tranquility," could not have been made and at the same time promote and maintain "a system of rapine and murder like slavery, especially as not one word can be found in the Constitution to authorize such a belief."

He had advised President Lincoln in 1862 to free the slaves in Washington, D.C., and understood that this fight was really versus an economic system directly in contradiction to the principles on which the country had been founded.

Now I know this doesn't make much sense, but all this week I have read and heard a lot regarding the celebration of the 200th anniversary of the birth of President Lincoln. In all of this, I have only heard Fred Douglass name mentioned briefly once, but the repeating mantra of the Lincoln-Douglass debates are batted around like they were the real debate of his time. No, the real debate was between he and Douglass, for it was Douglass, in his interaction and dialogue with Lincoln that had the greatest impact in the long run.

### 27 - Thursday, February 21, 2008

One thing about America, a racist or supremacist is not that far away. Maybe a keystroke away, or maybe a channel away. Bu they are always around. Over the past week, I was in dialogue with such a person. But that is all I will say to that extreme. However, I can deal with the aforementioned since his audience is not that Large.

On February 19, 2008, during his radio talk show, FOX news host Bill O'Reilly took a call from a program listener regarding the wife of Senator Barack Obama. The caller said that according to a close friend of Michelle Obama, that she was "a very angry," and "militant woman."

The segment of the show of course was focused on her comments regarding being proud to be an American for the first time in her adult life. I wouldn't expect Billy, or the average white band, I mean listener to understand what she meant. But I do and did; I mean folk here saw national guards on his street telling him he couldn't play outside. I'm certain that it is out of left field for Billy or his caller to understand that some folks do remember segregation (albeit) I don't, and taught it to their children. They may remember their parents having dogs set on them, or water hoses unleashed on them with their full fury, or how whites acted when the first school buses transported black kids to predominantly white Boston schools, or Bombing of the 16th street avenue church.

Some whites may not remember that their parents may have taught them that they couldn't vote and had to ride in the back of buses for the same fair, or having to have separate waiting rooms, entering the back of establishments or drinking out of different water fountains. Maybe they think that folks of my persuasion ethnically should be proud of that as an American – nope, we are not. I mean, to my recollection, we never enslaved whites, or set dogs on them, or bombed their churches when maybe some felt that they needed to be bombed

In his response, O'Reilly opined: "I don't want to go on a lynching party against Michelle Obama unless there's evidence, hard facts, that say this is how the woman really feels. If that's how she really feels -- that America is a bad country or a flawed nation, whatever -- then that's legit. We'll track it down. "

I don't know why I listen to him, but I think it is because I feel he is intrinsically divisive for America, and the enemy of mine, my folk and America. Last I heard it was illegal to lynch or assert that one would do such to a person in America. In fact, the House passed anti-lynching legislation three times in the first half of the 20th century. Dang, it wasn't until 2005 that America manned up and apologized for the historic acts of lynching on its shores

I would like to suggest that if you all can, please contact Bill O'Reilly, your congresspersons, senators and local law enforcements and hold him accountable for his words, I'm down for free speech, but saying lynching is ok with evidence, is like saying fire in a crowded movie theater to me. So why do you expect her to forget her lessons, God knows I don't and won't.

## 28 - Tuesday, February 26, 2008

Albeit my foreign policy experience has been limited to running child survival, maternal health and infectious disease risk reduction in prisons, and outside of the frequently penned essay on international affairs issues regarding politic and health, I am a novice. Maybe one reason why I would not be suitable for political office – add that my salacious selection of vocabulary and my predilection for women. That aside, I have reduced the political problems of Iraq into a workable solution. True I do not live there and like the US government, neither have I consulted or requested their approval of my executive order.

I have written extensively on the current circumstance that have placed us at war, from the President, to Don Rumsfeld, Neo-cons (even though have found a neo neocon), Pakistan, Afghanistan and even other assorted variables. But truth be told, we as a country, no matter how long we stay, or how many troops we can deeply, can't do nothing for the country, the people and the puppet government – I mean democracy we elevated in Iraq.

But If I were afforded the opportunity to use a Republic like a Monarchy this is what I would do. Given my previous failures at attempting to institute an artifact of imperialism, I would look toward the North and away from the green zone and other places I have made desolate with bombs and bullets. I would sit down with all of The Kurds, the Shiite and Sunni and talk about what was going on in that region. I

45

would tell them that, "As a nation they now have to be self-determined. That no matter where enemies come from, this could be a start for a unified Iraq." I would advocate that they all join forces and go to war against Turkey. This would accomplish our goal. We could bring our troops home and unify the country.

In my rally cry I would add, "The North is where most of the love is, and if we can destroy your country under the guise of false stockpiles for oil, then you can unify your blood for oil and for our nation. I figure this will finally unify Iraq and start the rebuilding of a unified nation state, unfortunately like it was under their former leader.

But that why I am not a politician. I don't know if the rest of my government would go for it, I mean giving those planes, as I did Turkey also. But it would work, and we could have all of our people home and watch out two allies in the region square off. This would be a job well done. LOL

## 29 - Saturday, March 01, 2008

Just finished reading the International Narcotics Report released by the State Department today (2.29.08). I tell you, the Taliban got it going on and it seems to be all charged by the hate of US – the United States and the West. According to the report:

"Narcotics production in Afghanistan hit historic highs in 2007 for the second straight year. Afghanistan grew 93 percent of the world's opium poppy, according to the United Nations Office on Drugs and Crime (UNODC). Opium poppy cultivation expanded from 165,000 ha in 2006 to 193,000 ha in 2007, an increase of 17 percent in land under cultivation... The export value of this year's illicit opium harvest, $4 billion, made up more than a third of Afghanistan's combined total Gross Domestic Product (GDP) of $11.5 billion. Afghanistan's drug trade is undercutting efforts to establish a stable democracy with a licit economic free market in the country. The narcotics trade has strong links with the anti-government insurgency, most commonly associated with the Taliban. Narcotics traffickers provide revenue and arms to the Taliban, while the Taliban provides protection to growers and traffickers and keeps the government from interfering with their activities. During recent years, poppy production has soared in provinces where the Taliban is most active."

Now this tells me a few things. 1] the 32,000 troops we got in Afghanistan have not been able to reduce the opium trade nor convince farmers to stop growing Poppy in the region and 2] if they will blow up 2000 year old Buddhist statues out the side of mountain, they won't stop until they blow up all of our troops.

Now this means that the Taliban is rolling in loot, 11.5 billion dollars' worth. I know I would if I sold more than 90% of all the stuff that was the primary ingredient to make heroin. And I know, my senior chemistry seminar paper was how to make heroin #10 from Morphine (and I still got a copy, of which dude gave me an 89).

My main point of consternation is that the locations where cultivation of Poppy is the greatest is in areas that's under the NATO forces' control. So in essence, the Taliban is using this money to attack US and NATO forces as well as the U.S. backed government. The report is called the U.S. State Department's annual International Narcotics Control Strategy Report. A Briefing on the report was given by Assistant Secretary David T. Johnson

We turned a blind eye to the plant when the Taliban was being funded and supplied by US when they were considered a way to make inroads into the country in 1979. But we can't blame them, because it easy money since I suspect that all the Taliban has to do is provide protection to growers and traffickers to collect. We supposedly reduced their power in 2001 but today still in 2008 we are locked in fierce battle with them folk.

All we do is talk about eradication of the plant when we know good and damn well that eradicating opium hurts already super, duper poor farmers. Meaning we talk about crop replacement but what crop gone replace the kind of loot that poppy can generate? Coca or weed maybe, but not olive trees for sure. In 2003 it was estimated that poppy production according to the International Monetary Fund, accounted for 40 percent to 60 percent of the Afghan economy. So now I am speculating, since we have been there it now represents about 70 to 75% - is that an increase?

Here at home, heroin has made a comeback, albeit as LL Cool J said, "been here for years." Based on data reported in the National Household Survey on Drug Abuse, there are an estimated 3,091,000 U.S. individuals 12 years of age and older that have used heroin at least once. Now even kids are being hooked on the stuff. In Texas for example, there has recently become a large corpus of kids as young as 11 getting hooked on the stuff. Really they are becoming addicted to a mixture of heroin and Tylenol PM, commonly called "cheese." News Reports suggest that they buy it at school with their "lunch money and snorted it through hollowed-out ballpoint pens."

I guess this will be another legacy of G.W. Bush. I mean, we supposedly making progress at least in the strong hold of the Taliban. But what do they do, they take us down with one stone, growing poppy to supply their military wing, and get our youth, the future military persons of our country, addicted to the same shit.

### 30 - Monday, March 10, 2008

Jones main, you folk here grew up around dice. I used to love to see Earl Campbell (3/4) come up on the first roll. But I had to let it go after the night my boy Hotrod got stabbed in a dice game over a side bet. Had to sneak him in the house after his folks went to sleep. Think it was 10th grade.

Now days, Hillary Clinton sound like she shoot dice. She is always taunting her 35 years' experience. So I have been doing some thinking, If she is 60 now, that means she been in public service since age 25, which I find hard to believe. Sure a large amount of that time was as first lady of Arkansas and the First Lady of the United States, but really, outside of that, what experience does she have?

I know in the late 1970s, when she worked with the Rose Law firm, I have read that she opened a commodities account with $1,000 and was able to Parle that into $100,000 365 days later. But that's beside the point, the Law firm, which I couldn't find no mention of on her website, was infamous for scandal after scandal including "Whitewater; the death of Vince Foster, a Rose partner who became deputy White House counsel; and the missing billing records from Rose that were discovered in Hillary Clinton's book room at the White House."

Whitewater enabled the Clintons to sale Arkansas real estate. Although Hillary stated on the record that, as an attorney at the Rose Firm she was not significantly involved in the representation of "Jim McDougal's savings and loan, Madison Guaranty." However, billing records documented that she had billed Madison for 60 hours of work over a 15-month period as covered in a PBS special a while back.

My issue is that she brags on all these years of experience. She has only been in the senate 7 years and the way I see it, being first lady of a state or the country is ceremonial – she was not voted and we had to take her as his wife without question.

I do know that while in the White house and over Health Care Reform, she cost us about $13 million. Then there was her small role in being allowed to select an Attorney General. Her first two recommendations (Zoe Baird and

Kimba Wood) did not make the cut and were forced to withdraw their names eventually leaving her to name Janet Reno. Bill Clinton considered Reno to be his "worst mistake.'

It doesn't stop there because she also advocated that her former law partners, Web Hubbell, William Kennedy and

Vince Foster, for positions in the Justice Department, the Treasury and as a Whitehouse staffer. We now know that Hubbell was later imprisoned, Foster died under strange circumstance, and Kennedy was forced to resign. In her experience, she also got her husband to pardon some clients of her brother's (Hugh & Tony) in exchange for hefty campaign contributions. These included Carlos Vignali Jr. who was convicted in 1995 in Minneapolis for moving 800 pounds of cocaine and Edgar and Vonna Jo Gregory for a 1982 Bank fraud convictions

As the Senator from NY, she has not even promoted nor passed any significant – at least that I can find on the books, I may be wrong. But outside of any of the aforementioned, she has only worked at law firms (one for 15 years) and been a wife to a governor and a president. She even talks about her foreign policy experiences, when I read in the New York Times once that "one meeting with mutilated Rwandan refugees so unsettled her that she threw up afterward." What kind of leader does that?

Add to that, some of her positions just don't make common sense to have so much experience. First, she opposes the international treaty to ban land mines. She also voted against the Feinstein-Leahy amendment last September which restricts the U.S. exports of cluster bombs "to countries that use them against civilian-populated areas."

Now there is much more, but all I want to do is suggest that maybe her 35 years' experience is a big fib, and that maybe Mr. Obama needs to bring this to the fore. If I can find it, I know his folks can too. And it's not slinging mud, it's just factual and namely a function of how she comes up with the number 35 years and here positions and failed attempts in politics when she was first lady. Otherwise, if he don't she gone keep rolling the dice, talking about the Eighter from Decatur – for the none crap shooter, that's 3-5.

## 31 - Saturday, March 15, 2008
Now Jones, your folk here aint the richest man in the world, in fact I am one of the poorest. With that said, over the past two months I done lost a lot of loot. I kind of hoard loot and try to stay away from spending it if I do not have to, especially if I aint got it.

The current credit crunch is hitting everybody nowadays and I am not just talking about the financial institutions. I mean the common man, the banks, Wall Street, Japan, and even Europe. I know people are doing all they can to ameliorate these problems, but suffice it to say, it will be hard to fix when the average person doesn't have, and has a desire to spend, even when they do not have the money on hand. I feel I have the right to complain about the government practicing deficit spending, but those that do such themselves do not.

What I anticipate next is that Banks and Brokerage houses (one in the same since Clinton abrogated Glass-Stegall), which have already been hit hard by the subprime lending practice and home mortgage losses, are not going to being seeing the good times any time soon. Since August of last year, the U.S. government has given financial institutions nearly a trillion dollars and things have yet to improve. Now the Federal Reserve Bank is getting into the act and is talking about allowing banks/brokerage houses to exchange mortgage-backed securities (MBSs) for about 200 billion in Treasury bonds. Talking about shooting dice, I mean, the have never accepted MBSs as collateral before – not to my knowledge. This will make the FR a holder of long-term credit risk. I figure the FR doesn't need to do this for it is the financial and lending institutions that need to make corrections on their practices and get their shit tight.

We already see our trade deficit increasing. Especially as it relates to exports as a function of being offset by higher oil prices. It increased almost $60 billion last month alone, and the increase specifically with China seems to grow more and more each day.

So in summary, it is the value of the dollar that is essential to a strong economy in the US. I do not like losing money, not even in the washing machine, and over the last 60 days I have lost $11,071.27. My problem is if I can see this, not as an economists, why can't our government?

## 32 - Wednesday, March 19, 2008

Addiction is a very serious disease (yep disease). Just like depression and/or cancer, it disables the body in various fashions and can be stimulated prior the consumption of any substance such as cocaine and alcohol, or via disruptions in cyclic AMP pumps or varying levels of naturally occurring chemicals in the body such as enzymes and neurotransmitters.

Now I know a many of bloggers have touched on a few speeches recently, in particular the one delivered by Barack Obama. However, it was really something I could not attend to since it was based on old news, albeit I was asked to consider writing about it by some of my fellow bloggers. I did not for it would have been a short brief; one that would have advocated that he listened to School House rock too as a child.

Today, our recovering addict in chief, President George W. Bush, addressed the Pentagon in honor (if it can be considered a celebration) of our fifth year anniversary of our invasion and occupation of Iraq. To me considering such as an anniversary is like celebrating the coming of the plague.

In his first speech, in 2001, which I have only read and not heard, he made several statements that stuck out like a hard dick. He made a few statements that stuck with me. The first was "One by one, we are eliminating power centers of a regime that harbors al Qaeda terrorists." Moreover he added that "Enemies of America have now added to these graves, and they wish to add more."

This time, he did the same, and like an addict, it appeared as if he was intentionally misleading or even lying to the America public. He said that "The tasks that remain in Iraq - to bring an end to sectarian conflict, to devise a way to share political power and to create a functioning government that is capable of providing for the needs of the Iraqi people - are tasks that only the Iraqis can complete."

I find this strange since first, the sectarian conflict that he speaks of did not start till expost facto our invasion and next because the violence that is sectarian, has been mainly promulgated by our policy – namely of paying insurgents and militias that are apart of Awakening Councils, to protect each neighborhood. Now Iraq may as well be like Compton, California, where each block is maybe controlled by some set of Crips or Bloods. In Iraq, especially Baghdad, each neighborhood is controlled by their own militias, who we pay, like sects, to war against each other neighborhood.

Mr. President also suggests that: "…for the terrorists, Iraq was supposed to be the place where al-Qaida rallied Arab masses to drive America out. Instead, Iraq has become the place where Arabs joined with Americans to drive al-Qaida out. In Iraq, we are witnessing the first large-scale Arab uprising against Osama bin Laden, his grim ideology, and his terror network. And the significance of this development cannot be overstated."

This too is strange since the CIA and his own military and other assorted advisors admitted that Al Qaida was not operating in Iraq when Sadaam was in power. In particular given that they wanted to see his form of government abrogated and replaced with a theocracy – meaning he was a thorn in the side of Al Qaida and observed as their enemy, an infidel. And again, the only way one could say that Arabs are working with the American military is to say that the 1) assist with maintaining the roughly 2hr of continuous electricity they have a day when before the war it ran uninterrupted and 2] that accepting payola from the US military, to use insurgent groups to protect their neighborhoods and battle with other neighborhoods is considered the definition of working together with the US military.

For a person that doesn't live in or visit Iraq regularly, it is unintelligible to cognize how he can make such a denouement. As a scientist, I can't use a single indicator to mark such a consummation. For it appears to me that the only one he is using is the number of death, or the reduction of deaths thereof. The killer was the catch phrase of how it ended up being "The battle in Iraq has been longer and harder and more costly than we anticipated" – like I am supposed to believe he gave this war serious ideation in the first place – LOL.

To me, they only difference from the first speech and this one today was that back then, by his side, well almost was his distant cousin of the executive office, Senator Hillary R. Clinton. In addition, I guess today he was trying a wag the dog and remove all of the attention from the fucked up economic position his deficit spending war-mongering ass has facilitated. All in all, I just know he said we would triumph and that I have yet to get the rose garden he promised. And meanwhile, Mr. 100 year war - John McCain (albeit he is old enough to have been in the war between France and England), is in Israel, campaigning, like it is a state in the US.

## 33 - Sunday, March 30, 2008

I know a lot of folks will likely vilify my character, what little I maintain, after I say this. Snitching is cool with me, especially if u owe me loot or if u aint seeming like you gone pay up. But then again what would you expect, I am the kind of person that will tell folks where to find me if I say what they don't like or consider to be appreciate.

So yea, I'm a snitch and will tell with the quickness, for I can only be accountable for my own dirt and no one else's. But like most black folk, the government aint down with snitching. After the largest recall of beef and beef-by products (Vienna sausages and potty meat with veins and the likes), the Agriculture Department is considering a measure that would allow for them not to tell the folks affected by such – the public, the names of retailers that may have and may have sold tainted to said aforementioned public.

As it stands, the USDA doesn't not release or publish or list the names of food retailers that might have received or sold meat that may be hazardous. This means that if you happened to buy some of this carcinogenic mutated shit, there is no way for you to know if the store you got it from got their meat from one of the slaughter houses putting mad cow disease on the refrigerated isle at low low prices.

I mean this ain't a small deal, we talking about 143 million pounds of beef. Supposedly the argument is that they fear full disclosure will result in pressure applied to the companies that process and manufacture mad cow and e coli tainted beef. I'm like tell, who gives a hoot? Tell and tell all.

In 2007, United Food Group LLC recalled 445,000 pounds based on "unspecified concerns" raised by the California State Department of Health Services which had been shipped to stores in Arizona, California, Colorado, Idaho, Montana, Nevada, New Mexico, Oregon, Utah, Washington and Wyoming. I must admit, after some added pressure, the USDA have released the name of the districts impacted by this latest recall, but that's about it. Like a mother fucka know what district his meat comes from like it's a voting or school district or something.

Laws protecting the public good are already super permeable, I mean how else such meat (about 50.3 million pounds worth) could could get into school lunch programs around the country – yes Atlanta being one. So I'm asking yawl to "reconsider, read some literature on the subject" because I love me some meat, and wanna know who got what I purchase frequently, and from where they got it. So promote snitching, say that snitching is good my people. Sure I trust my stomach acids and gastric enzymes, but I still don't want to eat a tainted steak, that may have anything in it from mad cow to toxic shock (arm above). Cooking I don't think, kills either.

### 34 - Monday, April 07, 2008

Ok, Jones, main, your folk been putting in some work, albeit I feel I aint got to tell you that. I mean it's just what I do. But it has been good. I was working with an interior designer, but she was talking crazy for a store for dogs, like it was some retro chic Lenox Mall boutique. I had someone else before her, but it aint pan out. But that being said, the ruminations have still been going on. I admit, I have been trying to stay away from the primaries, but it's hard so I am going to drop this on you – thanks to a conversation with Kelso, UCLA, rooting against Memphis monkey ass. Otherwise, like I said, it has been good, not because around this time at age 13, Shakespeare penned his first play, which turned out to be Romeo and Juliet, but because I have ratcheted the fortitude to write about politics once more and because Memphis throttled UCLA.

I have wondered to myself who would, will or would make the best running mate for Barack Obama. This is especially true since the mantra of the Clinton team is experience,

experience and experience. It seems they talk and hammer the experience card more than her plans to deal with the recession or the conflicts abroad in Asia (Afghanistan and Iraq).

Unfortunately as the reader may expect, I will not take the "most electable ticket" route. Instead, I have dug deep in the shallow capacity of my brain to figure out what would make the most appealing and winnable ticket. I know the pundits have mentioned a few names, and some of them make sense to me.

The names that I have heard thus far include Senator Bill Bradley, Senator Russ Feingold, Governor Bill Richardson, Senator Chris Dodd, Senator Jack Reed, General Wesley Clark and last but not least, former Presidential hopeful Senator John Edwards. Sure there have been others including Governor Brian Schweitzer, Governor Kathleen Seibulus and Congressman John Murtha, but the last three don't really cut the cake, especially Murtha with his history or shady political dealings.

However, I must admit there are some strong benefits to some in the first group. Bradley once ran for the presidency, and has strong name recognition, not to mention the championship ring he won when playing with the New York Knicks back in the day. Add to that, he could help him carry New York, thus he has a serious upside. Feingold, well she is known for her work with the Republican winner, John McCain. For me, she has done enough damage to McCain from the way many in the GOP see it and thus, cannot add anymore by being on the Obama ticket. Bill Richardson has more up than down as well. Not only can he assist with the Hispanic vote, he also is a good man to provide some experience on Defense, AIDS and the economy. Then there is Governor Kathleen Seibulus of Kansas. She would help carry white women and would likely bolster Obama's policy positions on energy, education and the environment.

I could talk about them all but like the above, I'd be talking about shit folk already know. This is why I don't see any of the above being able to give Obama a winning ticket, electable yes, winning no. So I suggest that as a running mate, Obama select Colin Powell. Yes former Secretary of State and Head of the Joint Chiefs of Staff Colin Powell. Obama is the ma to do it and it would definitely show up John "McCain/Feingold" McCain what reaching across the aisle really is. America would love it and bam. White house folk.

Now you may laugh and suggest such is farfetched, but I want to recount the serious amount of thought, wandering thought I have put into this since December. In fact in my book, it's an essay called remember this name, about Obama, written in 2004 that predicted he would run successfully for the democratic nomination – even against my libertarian sensibilities.

The Harlem born Powell is a Vietnam veteran. On his this second tour he was injured in a helicopter crash yet still was able to rescue his peers from the burning helicopter. For this he was given the Soldier's Medal. He has a MBA from George Washington University and even served as Secretary of Defense and National Security Advisor, under President Ronald Reagan.

So laugh all you want, but this is the winning ticket and don't play the lottery. Show your hand folk, give me one better. In wrestling this would be called a pile driver, but I refer Powell Driver. Cause if he doesn't, McCain will likely have Condi Rice as his.

### 35 - Sunday, April 20, 2008
These rickety splitting politicians, including Obama, talk about health care as if it is an easy problem to solve. All like I said have put of some big-worded proposals on the table that sound delicious in sound bit form on the surface. Clinton REQUIRES all citizens to have coverage versus Obama's

plan to start with children first. In addition, I have noticed that a thorough review of McCain's plan (although he use the Mantra of Obama now which is making health insurance more affordable) sounds like he is dealing with a telephone monopoly by suggesting his goal is to foster more competition in an effort to reduce costs and improve the delivery of services. He also wants to provide folks with a refundable $2,500 tax credit as an incentive to buy insurance.

Similar to McCain, Hillary Clinton plan also focuses on lowering costs and improving quality. I find the latter with respect to both McCain and Clinton as being feculent given that America has the best health care in the world. So to me, improving the quality of our health care misses the point.

Although I believe the Obama's plan is the most practical and comprehensive (not hard for a c minus to beat 2 D pluses), he too misses the point on the general issues at hand. As I read his prospectus, he is more concerned about specifics such as mental health, Autism, AIDS and Mercury Pollution. True, he as Clinton and McCain want to expand research and place the Insurance companies in check, they still don't seem to have a veridical or pragmatic approach to health care.

Truth is none of these folks running for president seem to notice the wide range of cost for the same procedures across states and even hospitals in the same states. Using me as an example, which I think is most folks, know who offers the best service in anything and who has the lowest prices. As a consequence, folks tend to go, and are willing to drive to those institutions that have both and the politician's plans do not address this. Moreover, none even talk or mention the fact that there is a very demanding shortage of Nurses and physicians in America. They also do not deal or address the fact that medicine and health care is being run by business men as opposed to physicians and scientist - foul. That's like having Wall Street run by a maid to me.

I know many folks say that health care is a privilege as opposed to a right and accordingly, some folks really believe that only people who can afford health insurance should have it. Such a premise is primitive to me. I mean, what will these folks say 20 years from now when there is a worldwide food shortage? Will they say that only people who can afford food deserve to eat? We are talking about mainly people who are working and still can't afford health care or the massive deductibles required before the benefits of insurance kick in. Having universal health care will not do anything and may not even help. So big wig politicians, revamp, and focus on trying to get more folks insured as opposed to all folks. By doing the previous it is easier to accomplish the latter. Otherwise we will be in the same boat and with respect to health, America will never join the rest of the civilized world.

### 36 - Tuesday, April 22, 2008

For those of you who don't know, I used to teach ancient African History. Although it was supposed to start from 200 B.C.E. (before Christian Europe) to 1100 A.C.E. (after Christian Europe), I started it during the time of the Djebel Ouenat carvings in Libya during the Upper Paleolithic age as well with a brief introduction of the Gloger Law. If you are not familiar with the latter, simply stated it postulates that warm-blooded animals need to be pigmented in hot climates. This means as a primer, folk started the class with a brief overview of the origin of man from Homo habilis to Homo erectus to Homo sapiens sapiens.

I did this although my main interest in history was during the periods of colonialism and slaver (of which a lot seems to overlap). Slavery for me holds both emotion and disdain. I was even asked and authored several historical pieces for the World Encyclopedia of slavery. Particularly on the punishment of slaves, the Kansas Nebraska Act and Church Schisms Slavery. I can't see for the life of me how a group of folk can be so lazy and evil to place another (with or without their assistance) in bondage. It just confuses the shit out of me. Moreover, it really trips me out how some may suggest that it was not "that" bad, or that it is over and happened hundreds of years ago. Such a position pisses me the fuck off too.

It is as if they don't see capitalism and racism as being the same thing as formulated in slavery. It is as if they don't see how years of perpetual servitude without profit can have a devastating impact on the psyche, soul and more importantly pocket of the one enslaved. I really would love to see someone today work for Sears, or Wachovia or U.S. Steel for their entire life and not receive a penny, get am benefit or pension from said years of effort.

The way I see it, the proclamation announced by Lincoln really did not free the descendants of Africa. Sure it enabled them to move away from pimps called slave masters, but it was not freedom. For freedom has to be pursued aggressively. It is like Julius K. Nyerere said "Freedom too many means immediate betterment, as if by magic. Unless I can meet at least some of these aspirations, my support will wane and my head will roll just as surely as the tickbird follows the rhino."

It was really, as Douglass Blackmon called it a new time and more so the start of the "Age of Neoslavery." A period where folks could still enjoy slave labor without the title of "slavery" attached. Just as the Jim Crow laws or the Black Code statutes passed to maintain white control after the Civil War, today, the same form of slavery exist except without the chains, torture and punishment. Just as then, current laws are designed and put in place to intimidate African Americans, namely males because they were able to do rigorous free labor.

Yes I am talking about prison, and really since the freedom of slaves. But this is not important, because it is

61

over and it had no impact on the current condition of Africans in America today. But I bet if you asked U.S. Steel, Tennessee Coal (Pratt Coal & Coke Co.), the Georgia and Alabama Railroad, U.S. Pipe & Foundry (Jim Walter Corp/ Walter Industries) or Sloss-Sheffield Steel & Iron Co among a lot of other major corporations that I won't name, they aint willing to give back the money they stacked as a function of free labor. But then again it was prison labor; labor not protected by the Fair Labor-Standards Act. Just as today, a many folk end up in prison due to stupid shit that is exacerbated by ridiculous sentences and ridiculous fines. It just seems that it is deliberately directed mathematically disproportionately to African Americans, and it amazes me how folks can even say that the insidious legacy of racism called slavery doesn't reverberates today.

Yes, convict leasing is still really real, but no longer in the South, as in days of old but rather nationwide. They don't keep records anymore, but back in the day it was estimated that the Alabama's forced-labor system made $17 million for the state government alone (about 250 million in today's dollars).

My thing is this, if it was not cool for Hitler to force Jews to work in a similar form, and they were awarded loot for making German corporations rich, why the double standard? As far as I am concerned, U.S. Steel is still using us, I mean they still making profit of the loot, ain't they, like the others. I'm through.

### 37 - Sunday, April 27, 2008
Normally I would have probably written a little something on penal politics in honor of Sean Bell. However, my mundane expression could do little if any more given the inordinate post I have read on this since the verdict was passed down. But it is like what did one expect? This is America, this is not a democracy- what did you expect (this is why studying

history is important, for it tells us we should have expected such)?

Instead, I am reminded of the time when I used to play games, all kinds of games from four square, to any sport, to kickball and checkers and chess. But there was one game I could never get, and the strange thing was that seemed like me and all my friends had it - Chinese checkers. Now I may be sating myself but it came with every game of checkers ever sold.

To connect the dots, I keep hearing that the Cold War is over. Maybe it is, maybe it isn't. I do know that they, Russia, formerly the USSR does not exist anymore. But if you asked me - which no one has, I would like to suggest that the cold war is alive and kicking.

Just like Dusty Rhodes versus Ric Flair, the U.S. and China have been locking horns and doing battle like it was for a championship belt. And it seems as if China is winning, or at least has the upper hand. Starting with the yuan and the way they have pegged the currency to how they assist in creating higher gas prices based on us being one of the biggest exporters of refined oil to them; and don't even mention how they crushed our steel industry back in the day. But I won't get into that for its enough new info on the latter for food for thought.

Now aside for the "knock this off my shoulder shit", like picking on them for Tibet and Darfur, or them picking on us because of Iraq, there is some major stuff going on that I never see and barely read in the news - I guess that's a function of having a zillion debates and candidates saying the same thing over and over and such being considered news.

First it was their disagreement with the U.S. Steel energy report that suggested China had supported its steel industry with energy subsidies of 27.1 billion U.S. dollars from 2000-07. Thus why it was a big issue in the Penn primaries, given none of the democratic hopefully could thoroughly address the issue.

Yes, China is winning. Not only do they make bird flu, and scare the shit out of US and make toys and baby cribs that can be considered as booby traps that harm and mutilate, even kill our children, now they are hitting us with tainted drugs. According to the USFDA, there may be at least 81 deaths across the country that may be related to contaminated blood thinner made in China. The FDA has been engaged in a bitter battle with the Chinese government over this. The agency publicized that the active ingredient in Heparin sold by Baxter Pharmaceutical was contaminated at Chinese manufacturing facilities, with a dietary supplement made from animal cartilage called chondroitin sulfate. Heparin is a polysaccharide that is found in the human body with the greatest concentration in tissues around the liver. It is used to prevent blood clots from forming.

I tell you, the cold war is not over, I mean, just because the name of the enemy is changed, don't mean jack to me. So Like in *Ender's Game* by Orson Scott Card, we may need to learn how to fight the Chinese at their own game, maybe not with learning how to play video games as in the aforementioned book, but maybe by learning Chinese checkers, so get the kids ready folk.

### 38 - Tuesday, April 29, 2008

Last week I referred to Senator John McCain a few times. Namely because I wrote about him and his overzealous overview of economics and economic reform. Moreover because his depiction doesn't match my understanding of mathematics, as limited as it is. Also, because I could not post such given the incessant tags I was getting. Truth be told I have a major disdain for this thing they call "tagging" and don't like math either – I just know how to do it proficiently.

But before I go any further, I would like to say (1) Reverend Wright put it down in Detroit at the NAACP dinner, (2) George W. Bush is a funny cat at least what I can suppurate from his speech he gave at this year's annual White House Correspondents Association dinner and (3) I love the LSU new baseball uniforms, throwback, Negro League style.

But Back to McCain, I have a basic difference with his math and fundamental approach to economics. I mean, I finally got a look at some semi-specifics regarding his pompous assertion that he will be able to end the budget deficit by the end of his first term as president - like he gone get in office and have a second term at that.

I feel that getting in office is going to be hard. First he has basically a financial vote of no confidence from the GOP seeing he has only raised about 3 million dollars for the general election. Meaning to me he will likely have to give all that loot back and accept federal funding to compete with Hillary (who has raised about 21 million) or Obama (who has raised about 8 million) for the general election slated for this November. As it stands now, Obama has 42 million available for the remanding primaries and Hillary has about 8 million. However she has debts accrued during the primaries of about 10 million dollars. Rule of thumb, if a candidate for the presidency is in debt during the primaries, how can one take their economic plan for the country serious?

But McCain, in one word is scary. He in his economic proposal is proposing a spending cut that will amount to about one third of the annual domestic budget. The package asserts about 600 billion dollars in cuts, however most of the compensation will be directed toward corporations and upper income earning households. Thus programs like education, student loans, social security and Medicare will have to lose a lot of loot if what he has proposed is to take place. My problem is that Jones aint even said what he will cut - and it would be wise for him to tell me before the elections if he is going to be "straight talking" to the general electorate. Not to mention, folk say he gone do all of this while at the same time increasing the size of the military. This tells me that more money will be required for his 100 year war and more money will be needed to increase the military with respect to service personnel, support staff and equipment.

McCain is giving a new meaning to Draconian if you asked me. In fact I think from now on, in concert with his Mcainanomics and 100 years in Iraq, he has given a new epitaph to laws that can be considered exceedingly harsh; very severe - Draconian. But then again I'm a poor black man with a feeble vocabulary, so what would I know?

### 39 - Monday, May 12, 2008

I am always amazed at the vehemence and disdain that many in the west have directed towards the Arab nations of the world and even their religion. It is difficult for me to understand this in many respects. Sure I am aware of (911 and of the recent wars and invasions that we have taken the liberty to impinge upon these countries, their citizenry and the culture of these folks). However, in many respects, it is unjustified, for I feel that there is no right for us to be so hateful towards a people unless our history was one that had no hate present at all. I mean, why be so vile toward folks because of one event?

Now having a total dislike for one's government and their policies is one thing, but a group of people for their beliefs, or because their beliefs are juxtapose to ours is plain old foul.

I know some would say that these are folks that will send women and children, with bombs around their bodies to blow up innocent people. True, But I recall that her in this country, the same occurred, when General Amherst gave Indians blankets infected with Small Pox. Now we over here

66

venerate Jones and have even named a prestigious university after him and a major city in New York. Although Jeffery was officially an English Lord by my recollection of history, he was the one that first introduced germ warfare. I know of this via reading Carl Waldman's Atlas of the North American Indian. In the book, while referencing a siege of Fort Pittsburgh by Chief Pontiac's in1763, he pointed out that General Amherst had via letter, suggested to Captain Simeon Ecuyer to give the Indians smallpox-infected blankets and handkerchiefs (BTW this started an epidemic among them

I can continue and I will because the Indian Boarding Schools were just as bad as the schools we criticize in Saudi Arabia. They were designed to mandate forced assimilation as well as destroy the culture of Native Americans – it was always funny to me how a person can discover a place where people already live, talk about arrogance. These schools too were made popular by another American historic Icon of sorts - Richard Henry Pratt. Pratt started the Carlisle Indian School in 1879 and set the standards for such schools to follow. And just like the Muslims abroad, here Christian denominations were allowed to build them on reservations (thanks to another hero's peace plan - Ulysses S. Grant).

And like the Christian's were with Africans, their Christian like nature tended to display act more akin to: physical, mental, and emotional abuse that often resulted in death. From promoting poor sanitation and hygiene to washing Indian children in kerosene to prove their point – whit is the only way and right.

They would cut their long hair – the main reflection of their culture pride) had to where the clothes of the "white man." But I imagine the worse thing was being bound and beaten or even burned for speaking their language. And I won't even mention slaves. But if there is a point I am trying to make is, don't be so hateful for others because they are different and don't let the beliefs of a few produce generalizations to all. More importantly, don't have double stand-ards, be two faced or speak with a forked tongue for we all have dirt behind our ears.

## 40 - Wednesday, May 14, 2008

I hope that none of us forget that we got folk overseas bat-tling on two fronts: Iraq and Afghanistan. It seems some-times as if we do, myself included. Being more concerned with Nick Cannon marrying some singer or Bow Wow turn-ing drinking age, or even a trivial personal problem or a night out at the club with our folks or a woman acting out on a train because she has not taken her medication. But too, there is nothing wrong with that for different things hold the inter-est of different folk.

I just want to remind folks that aint nothing has changed, except we are myopic, and maybe more interested in folks in suites (Hillary included) running for political of-fice than the fact that folks are still returning home in plastic bags or maybe even alive, with their leg or arm lost some-where on a road in a place called Kirkuk or Kabul or Mosul or Tikrit. I would even speculate that most of us couldn't name five cities outside of the capitals of both countries let alone tell which of the aforementioned is not in Iraq. But our self-induced ignorance is a divagation I will save for another day.

Maybe our nescience is why we don't notice or hear about Osama bin Muhammad bin 'Awad bin Laden anymore. The way they talked him up, you would have though Jones was the New Dillinger or Baby Face Nelson – public Enemy number one. I don't even see his picture up in Post Offices. Once upon a time I did.

I just wonder why? I wonder if he is even mentioned in the back rooms of the Pentagon or White House any more. All I know is that we have not found him but boasted we will. This is not a slap in the face of our military personnel.

Nope we have some of the bravest, smartest and efficient service men and women in the world and will forever have such. They carry out their task with expert precision and do it without one complaint. Yes, they are true professionals, more so that I. However, I do wish they had some help on the behalf of military intelligence. Makes me think that the combination of both words is an oxymoron.

I know some folks say all black folk look alike, maybe the same is true for Arabs and Muslims, and maybe this is why they have yet to locate Osama. Then we know that Osama Jones is hiding in a remote region of Afghanistan, maybe even Pakistan. Both of which are places where we have goo-gobs of military personnel and the assistance of folk who supposed to be our allies.

Maybe I am wrong. But I don't think so. Like I said, the folk we have fighting on our behalf are smart, very smart. But military intelligence, the question is still up for grabs to me. I mean it did take them about 5 years to find Eric Rudolph and we knew where he was plus he was state side. It also took them 11 years to find the Uni bomber. Maybe I just think too much and just need to stop and have me a shot of Tequila with hot sauce.

### 41 - Friday, May 16, 2008

There once was a time when education, regardless of gender, race or economic status was valued more so than anything else. It was seen as the great equalizer and the one intangible that was attainable by everyone.

Today seems that the value for education has diminished greatly, and that the transformation of values as such has turned for the worse. I had conversation with my folk this morning about his. As usual we saw this from different angles. He suggested that the values have not changed; it was that people tended to finish college but would still have no job, so I was not as important as it used to be in past days.

My position was not based on securing jobs, but rather the value of pedagogy in general.

Although I do not remember the time when my mom and her siblings went to school, I do remember seeing pictures. First it had to be hell and high water for them to miss a day in school and second they always had books in their hands.

My grandma would always say she never went to school. She had to work and getting married at sixteen meant she placed her family first. But this was in the late 1930s – a few decades before Brown versus the Topeka Board of education.

Today, it seems to be just different. Told him that 70% of the young African American males that enter the 9th grade won't graduate or finish school with their peers. That means that only 3 out of ten graduate high school, at least on time. Because of this 70 percent, nearly 80 percent eventually drop out.

I consider this foul on two fronts. First is our disposition and concern of materialism in the form of objects versus what one produces with his mind. Add to that our inability to want to work hard and delay gratification for the attainment of easy money. The last front is governmental, being that more money is spent on subsidies for oil companies, big business and given to places like Israel and Pakistan than is spent on education with respect to our public schools and the pay of teachers and institutions of higher learning with the reduction of grants, student aid and loans for those interested in college.

Again, I'm just venting, and sad. I used to hate being one of the two or three African American male professors at Emory University. I felt like I had to represent all of the African American men in the world and could only kick it with the building and grounds crew outside of the two aforementioned professors. In my book, this 70 is not a C, but really an F.

## 42 - Tuesday, June 17, 2008

Politics to me is more than just the Election and Barack Obama. As such, a blogger that is, the media serves a major role in how I get mad at shit and re-evaluate what they regurgitate to me under the auspice of news and information.

If you ain't heard, the Associated Press (AP) has decided to give the business to bloggers who reference (not publish) their news reports. Even direct quotes from folks that they don't even own.

The way I see it, they should be happy folks linking to they bitch ass on line because it increases their exposure. Nothing I write comes from them with the exception of stories I may get from them that I provide a direct link to their site.

But again this is the age of the fk boy or as one blogger called it the bitch man, for they are complaining about direct quotes ranging from 39 to 79 words – a paragraph. I just don't see why they get to make or define what fair versus excessive usage is? The AP aint the courts and last I heard the courts define laws and not a single media conglomerate. I just say face it folk, this is the new media jones. Yawl basically obsolete with the exception of quote feeding. I mean that's what yawl do for them 1500 plus newspapers yawl get loot from. I'd figured they would be better served exposing the 2 U.S. senators, the two former Cabinet members, and the former ambassador to the United Nations who got point waived and lender fee waived loans from Countrywide Financial. But why pick on Senators Christopher Dodd (chairman of the Banking Committee) and Kent Conrad, of North Dakota (chairman of the Budget Committee and a member of the Finance Committee) , or former U.N. ambassador and assistant Secretary of State Richard Holbrooke when big fish like no named bloggers can be thrown in the frying pan? But then again, what do I know?

## 43 - Tuesday, June 24, 2008

Back in the day one would hear the word sequence and you would think about them little bitty azz circles with a hole in the middle that would be stitched together on a blouse, skirt or dress. Namely for women. I learned actually what this was, although I had seen them on clothes worn by my mom and granny, when I played the drums in the high school band because our majorettes (fine as they wanted to be) wore outfits made of them small circle things with the holes in the middle.

Not anymore, at least since Geneticists of Leiden University Medical Center have become the first folk to determine the DNA sequence of a woman. They say this was easier to perform on a woman since women do not typically have a Y-chromosome, but rather two X-chromosomes. Marjolein Kriek, a clinical geneticist working at the institute, is the first woman to have her genome sequenced, according to the University. They say it took those about six months to produce approximately 22 gigabytes of sequence data of lil momma.

I wanted to write this a while back since it happened in May because I wanted to see if I could verify if the findings confirmed Ohno's theory which estimated that the human genome must contain up to 100,000 distinct genes, since Human Genome Project found that humans today have only 20,000 to 25,000 genes. But I couldn't. But over all this has some far reaching implications. For one, if I were a geneticist, I would be making loot, charging the super-rich 200 stacks to have their genes sequenced. Then again maybe not, for a mind such as mind may find the fck boy gene, the bad breath gene, the liar gene or the lazy gene. And I don't need to give folks who have historically, like Carl Jung (who equated Africans to Gorillas and that "Living together with barbaric [lower] races [especially with Negroes] exerts a suggestive effect on the laboriously tamed instinct of the white race and tends to pull it down.") or Sir Francis Galton (the father of white supremacy in the form of eugenics) or even Darwin, any more ammunitions to berate and reduce people of Africa to the status of secondary organisms.

Even worse, they may be folk unlike me that may use this technology and information to play God and in the long run, represent the final step to engendering man made life – as skin stem cells. Any who, I thought it was interesting, and now sequence for me, no longer refers to the tine circles with holes in the middle stitched on dresses or skirts.

### 44 - Sunday, June 29, 2008

As many of you know, I'm forever calling folks out, even myself. I often use terms of endearment such as fk boy, or bitch azz to suppurate these thoughts into manageable constructs. Today I will use another term that I was familiarized with while growing up in Memphis – weak azz bitch. Now before I start, I want to say that this direct objectified gerund is neither race nor gender specific, and tends to be best exemplifying of collective acts that can be perpetrated by individuals or groups, for example the congress - especially the democratic members.

I have always been curious how folks can always say one thing and do another. Like the child that says they don't want to go outside, but cries when you don't let them out, or the woman that says she doesn't want to be with a certain man, but wants him after he has removed himself from her life, or as I have mentioned in the prior paragraph, a congress person who says they disagree with a certain policy yet supports it via vote.

Although unlike most of us, who just get a day off for the fourth of July weekend the Senate went home yesterday for the Fourth of July holiday without doing jack to deal with the pressing economic conundrums facing regular folk like us. All though the folk on both side of the aisle say they gone handle theirs, from my vantage point, they appear to act more like a gaggle of weak azz bitches.

Not only did the housing rescue bill could not proffer any love via a test vote, they also could not approve an electronic surveillance legislation to prevent physicians who accept Medicare (H.R. 6331: Medicare Improvements for Patients and Providers Act of 2008) from getting hit with a large percent pay cut. I mean it was passed in the house but filibustered in the Senate.

The only thing that these folks were able to do, I mean by a skunk measure (zero opposition votes) was the passing of a bill to fund the wars in Iraq and Afghanistan that also increases benefits for veterans.

I think the last measure was a good thing. However, it just strikes me as strange that all these democrats voted for this bill, but will likely go back home on the stump, to their districts and talk about how much money we wasting on this war effort. Talking about being two faced and slimy. I mean, it would be disingenuous for me, if I was a poly (many) trickster to say I disagree with all the loot going for the war effort as well as how it is being spent, but yet at the same time vote for the measure. The legislation, passed by a vote of 268-155, with Democrats logging 80 votes with republicans. I won't call any name this time, but you can find who voted for what here. But that's why I feel that this republic, for which it stands, seems to be more like an oligarchy each day – u know, "a government in which a small group exercises control especially for corrupt and selfish purposes" – namely staying in office and getting paid.

### 45 - Monday, June 30, 2008

I have been told that ignorance is bliss. I frankly disagree with this, but I have finally come across a case in which such may be factual and the case. We have suffered a rather harsh and disturbing 8 years under the current commander in chief.

We have seen high fuel prices, a dwindling economy, namely proffered by a reduced manufacturing base, lowering wages, and decline in the housing market and reduced purchasing power of the dollar. There are more I could add, including a costly war that was implemented for overzealous personal gain and/or fame and lowering academic performance across the board from primary school to college.

Yes, GWB has put his foot in it, basically unknowingly and via the suggestions of advisors that seem to have never had the best interest of folk like us in their hearts. I really feel sorry for the next president. I know it will be better in some form or fashion, but the road traversed will be arduous and difficult. Bumpy even with a many of moguls to avoid.

Yes, GWB, his legacy will be an assorted one. But for me, I will always recognize for his inept outcome regarding the current state of political affairs. For me even with the war and stagflation, I will always remember him as the great unifier. Yep, for this one man in his eight years has managed to do what others, even Martin King Jr. could not do. He has managed to bring together, whites and blacks, men and women, gay and heterosexuals, natural born citizens and immigrants, republicans and democrats. For we all know he must go. He has done all of this believe it or not unwittingly. So George W. Bush, I toast to you, leaving office and unifying America, for with you, your folk and your policies, we would not have been on the verge of this new possibility, of a man of African descent, taking residency in the white House.

### 46 - Sunday, July 13, 2008

This weekend I was doing my basic cowering of scientific journals from around the globe. For me this is like going to the club or bar hopping. It started because I had these two articles I had to proof for some journals that I wrote – BTW Cardiovascular risk reduction for African American men through health empowerment and anger management will be out soon in Health Education Journal, 67(3)208-218. Stephens et al (2008).

Any who, in my reading I went over the latest press releases from research facilities across the countries because shit like this never makes the newspapers. One that struck out involved the possible relocation of the Plum Island Animal Research Center.

Now I first heard of this place in a book, Silence of the Lambs. In the book the white FBI lady was talking to Hannibal Lechter and told jones that if he helped them catch the killer, he would be relocated to Plum Island. Plum Island is where the U.S. Department of Agriculture's Agricultural Research Service (ARS) in concert with the Department of Homeland Security and selected pharmaceutical companies are conducting research on foot-and-mouth disease (FMD) among other deadly animal toxins and viruses. Smart you would think to have such a research instillation on an Island true. But now, based the urging of The Department of Homeland Security, the Feds want to move the facility inland. Yep, inland for a research facility that holds the world's most contagious livestock diseases.

Plum Island is located approximately 2.5 miles from tip of Long Island a used to be run by the U.S. Department of Agriculture (USDA) until 2003, when the Department of Homeland Security took over. I just do not get how this could be safer in the eyes of supposedly people who got protecting the security of our country as their first mission. Can we learn anything from the British? I know we knew they were in Iraq for 27 years and eventually had to bail – lesson not learned. Also, there was an outbreak in Britain in 2001 – lesson obviously not learnt (spelling intentional) now this.

I mean from my minor background in infectious disease, I do know that FMD is way more (about 20 times) more infectious than smallpox. Add to that, FMD virus can be transferred via ones breath, saliva, mucus, clothes, or even a car. Sure it aint harmful to people – yet, but jones here eat meat. And I have not even attempted to calculate the economic impact on the country if an outbreak did occur – I like loot too much and the figures I produce may scare me.

The strange thing is that I just want to know what kind of scientist folk got working for them – the Department of Homeland Security and if I can get a job. Because I would never make a recommendation of such, not on my understanding of disease vectors or behavioral epidemiology, but based on what I know security to mean - freedom from danger. Don't these folk know they just giving terrorist ideas? Dang folk, now that is plum foolish.

### 47 - Monday, July 14, 2008

You know, before I actually had the chance to visit and live in South Africa for 4 summers in a row, I recant when Nelson Mandela was granted his freedom. As such I also recall when the first DEMOCRATIC elections were too be held. It was a major point of consternation for me because I knew just as the US; South Africa was a republic and not a democracy. As such, my folk was hating on Jones because he was down with the PAC as opposed to the ANC. I used to love their slogan – one settler, one bullet. But that is just the live free or die, don't tread on me, and Patrick Henry in Jones.

When I found out that TV-One was going to air the Democratic National Convention and Not the Republican National convention, I decided to modify the slogan proffered by the PAC to one TV, one bullet. Now don't get me wrong I aint hating on TV-one, but rather I am hating on their lack of acceptance that black folk in America only watch TV, are poorly informed and basically nowhere close to being well read. It made me mad. I mean we get mad at a satirical cartoon on the cover of the New Yorker but aint got the gumption to say shit bout stuff that keeps us stupid.

I mean, we need to see these mother fucas and what they actually propose so we can have a better understanding of the issues that we HOPE Barack Obama can handle if Jones wins the general election in November. I mean we already poorly informed and if we don't know the issues, or have tenable suggestions about how to solve the problem, then we can't or won't be able to tell if the answers we get from Obama or McCain are satisfactory or pragmatic. As a result, we will accept anything a mother fucker will tell us without objective and valid query. For me, that's foul. I already see problems equally in how both the front runners of both parties want to deal with the Economy and Health care. Not to mention they connections to K Street.

TV One should be ashamed to keep information from the community they say they care about. It is no different than saying since you black, you can't learn to read (you a slave). But then again what do folk here know, I'm just an Idiot Savant who is trying to become well read.

### 48 - Wednesday, July 16, 2008
I am an optimist true, but I have denied inside, that we can make it if we try, for I have failed to acknowledge that we ain't even trying. I am putting down what I am reading now to write what I'm finna (I'm country) write now. I only had about 45 pages of Pursuit: the chase, capture, persecution & Surprising Release of Confederate President Jefferson Davis. Really I have finished the text, I am just going through the 40 or so pages and 270 sum odd footnotes, to check the authors (Clint Johnson) interpretation of the events depicted - great read. In fact checking the footnotes is the best part of reading to me because you find out about other books. Any who, I'm finna stop because my blog rounds lead to such. And forgive me if I don't know when to stop because I'm listening to Chuck Brown and the Soul searchers "*Midnight Sun.*" Appropriate cause I hope I can make some of yawl search yawl

souls, which in my case is integrated with time, thought and the ability to reason.

We got to get out shit together folk. I mean, I went around the blogoverse over the last few days and all jones hear saw and read was either about Jesse Jackson, The cover of the New Yorker or Mr. Obama. Like dang folk, are we that myopic, limited in our intellectual sphere to consider such to be super important, as if these topics are all we can think about? Or as if they (these issues) were like melanin – super ferrous magnetic. Shit jones, folks could be about to start slavery back in affect and we on the hook, line and sinker tip still. What gives? When will we value free thinking and look for ourselves as opposed to respond to what other dangle in front of us. They say the Bass is a smart fish, but I never figured he was smarter than us. They don't bite at anything, even if it right in front of their face.

So your outrage over a satirical drawing or an obsolete former jones who ran for president is unwarranted, I mean is it important? Shole aint interesting. But get outraged while jones her say fck that shit mane. What does it do or what purpose does it serve? Chances are folks who think about Obama that way still and would have if they never did it. That don't do jack for me. So yawl go ahead, cause I'm more concerned about China, the Juan and global inflation. You see the way they control they currency rates, in concert with how fast their economy is growing may be bad for the world, especially US in the country of the New Yorker magazine.

I mean, in my junior high civics class, we talked about inflation and other stuff a lot albeit I don't know what Civics is to this day, I do recall the hodge podge of subjects it encompassed. From what I learned, if China keep on growing like they are, they can boost the current level of inflation elsewhere because the gone need more stuff (raw materials) to feed their growth.

Seeing that we in the US have cut interest rates, it's gone be hard for China to raise the value of the Juan – since it is pegged on the dollar. This means if oil don't come down, an increase in the value of the Juan would mean the stuff they send here that we buy like crack (cellphones, TV's. Cars, Steel, MP3 players and CDs) will make them a lot more expensive and hard for yawl to purchase. They done had the earth quake and some food shortages too – could be on like popcorn. Cause its already real in the field.

So Jones, don't think for me mane, or tell me what I am supposed see or feel when I read or see an image. Because I'm like, fk that shit, Midwest air lines just laid off 1400 workers and we don't know how many GM finna lay off. It's cool if yawl wanna be outraged over a magazine cover that I doubt many yawl read. Care about what impacts you for real though. So with that said, go find yourself some Chuck Brown and get that head right and soul search with the master. Otherwise, go and suck down some Juan Ton Soup, oh I mean Won.

### 49 - Thursday, July 17, 2008

I know a many are geared regarding the upcoming general elections to be held in November and regardless if you want Obama, McCain or Nadar to win, just do me one favor, ask them some well thought out and prospective questions regarding Afghanistan. Yep, I am about to bore you with another haterated triad.

I have come to accept that most folk don't get me jones. And when I say I don't give a fk bout certain things, they say I'm disrespectful or berating folks. So I am about to do more of the same. I feel that the ability to ask pointed questions, especially with respect to having some knowledge of possible solutions is the key to evaluating responses from any candidate for any office and or job. And for some reason or another, what's going on in Afghanistan scares the shit out of me.

Just last week it was reported that say about 200 Taliban fighters attacked a US military base located in the distant and mountainous northeast province of Kunar. They say it resulted in nine dead US soldiers and nearly a score of wounded. It aint been that many US military personnel killed in a single attack in more than three

For some reason, it appears that over the past seven months, the Taliban has gotten stronger, smarter and more brazen as opposed to what the current administration has been telling us. I mean it seem like it was just yesterday when folk was saying that they had accomplished victory and had won the war in this poppy growing country. Report released by the Pentagon on the situation, among other things said "the Taliban is likely to maintain or even increase the scope and pace of its terrorist attacks and bombings in 2008. The Taliban will challenge the control of the Afghan government in rural areas, especially in the south and east."

They say that this is a problem for the current administration; I feel that it is more of a problem for which ever jones steps in office after the elections in November. These attacks just aint on the outskirts, they like a hop, skip and a jump from the capital Kabul. The Capitol. And this recent attack was just one of many against a military base which they hitting up the regular now, not to mention it lasted all day. And this based had about 200 US troops. No little bitty convoy and it lasted all day.

When I do get a chance to hear what folks are talking about politically, they just be rehashing messages from stump speeches with little content. All I have heard Sen. Barack Obama say is that he will send two more combat brigades to Afghanistan and that he may take the troops from Iraq. All I know about Nadar is something he said 6 years ago regarding sending a small multinational force into Afghanistan to arrest

Osama bin Laden. McCain, well first he disagreed with Obama saying more troops were not needed; now he is copying Obama's position on the issue (u can read his flip flop history here at Obsidian wings, which is on my blog roll).

Like I said, I think we got to frame this issue and make it apart of the discussion, Iraq seems to get all of the attention, I am glad they TRYING to talk about the economy, albeit none from a global or international perspective in terms of problem solving (correct me if I'm wrong). Just talk of green Jobs and stuff like that. But about this small country, I'm not so sure, for at this rate, the Taliban will be in Kabul by December and in control of the government, again.

### 50 - Sunday, July 20, 2008

Now back to our regular scheduled thought crimes. First a disclaimer. I am no prognosticator as described by Fyodor Dostoyevsky in his Grand Inquisitor, nor do I own a 1-900 number or a crystal ball. Nor do I desire to see any harm come to anyone; unless they try to bum rush my shop or up on my 11 acres threatening me and mine, for I will bury them and they car.

But your folk just hit his global trip, first stop Afghanistan I think. Pundits say it is supposed to give clues about how he gone deal with foreign policy, particularly in the Middle East (aint no such place map wise it is Asia). Now what I am about to say is just me expressing brain cells that have yet to be depleted. Maybe it is my corpus of reticular formations or the inferior colliculus projections to the nuclei in my pons that are just as messed up. But this is it. I know the GOP are some dirt mother shut your mouths, especially after all the dirt they have slung at Obama courtesy of Mrs. Clinton. Knowing this one can see the desperation regarding winning this election in November at all and any cost. I hope I am wrong, but I just hope Obama watches his back while out of the country. These folks may plant a sniper somewhere in one of the countries where he is touring and just may try and take him out. That way, they could blame it on terrorist and attempt to gather more support for this mess we already in proffered by the neo Cons, and believe me you, I don't think the neo Cons would stop at anything to prove a point.

Not to mention the print media and TV has put this trip on front street unlike the trip made by McCain, which we barely heard a whisper about. So folk, if you folk read this blog man, watch your back. Ok, I'm through ruminating, don't get mad, like I said, thought and thinking arouses me so blame my Pons.

## 51 - Friday, July 25, 2008

Was gonna have another thought amnesty today since a many folk say I'm deep or that I think too much, or that I just plane ole hate when I go on my thought crime spree's. I was either gonna put up the speaking Memphisian #2 or Riddle me this #3. But I decided against such. As you read under point of order A, I have a penchant for paying myself. Now that said, I am reminded of how I have been taught what money was, how to use it and more importantly How to save it. Now I have not nor did I have a desire to watch the talking heads CNN producers aggregated for rating purpose, talk out the side of their necks about what I suspect many already know and experience. Not to mention the folks likely didn't repre-sent me nor my beliefs and that if it is on TV, it will eventu-ally, like in math, be reduced to the least common dominator of Entertainment.

Now of all folk, I know it's hard for the average per-son in America. I know that the value of the dollar aint like it used to be. I know that many of us struggle just to keep a roof over our heads – I know I do. But what I don't under-stand is how and why folks say it is hard and even difficult to save.

I mean it seems we have loot for what we want, but not what we need. Sure like I said it is hard, but not that hard. I figure that if a person goes out to a club or bar (which is cool) they will spend somewhere between 20 to $30 on the low end. That's reasonable. But if we do it twice a week or four times a month, that's about $2080 to $3120 a year in the first example and $960 tom $1440 a year in the second. Believe it or not that is a lot of loot if such habits persist for 3, 5, and 7 years – for which many of us do.

Sure you are or may say it is easy for me to talk, I got a PhD. True I do, but even before then I saved my money. Yea I invest, which think a lot more folk should do, and I see the volatility in the stock market, but I did so since high school and my family didn't teach me that. I aint never need a flashy car or nothing and I have never had a desire to go to a club and covet the VIP section nor make it rain on a stripper. If I did have the urge to make it rain, it would likely be on a homeless person or in homeless shelter.

Then we add to the problem, for we don't even recognize how our loot is degraded in meaning. We can go to a club and be made to pay valet parking, and pay $20 to get in when on the regular or for lack of a better descriptor – on white night, one can park they car and walk in free. We don't even complain, we just stand in line and pay. And don't let it be a party where some rapper or professional athlete gone be claimed to attend, then we just plum loose our fucking minds I guess what I am saying is that it's cool to enjoy life and make money, but it is not as hard as you think to save it. For although my folk aint invest or teach me how to, they did teach me how to save and that money was to make money and not to spend. Are we the only ones in capitalistic America that can't grasp this concept?

I'm hopeful everybody got they fix of CNN this past week, I'm sure they got some huge ratings. Unfortunately, I don't get down with talking heads and think they may be doing more to divide America than bring us together. I mean the title alone, sure there may be two three or four Americas, but I don't think a TV special does anything than tell folk what they already know and experience. Unless we live under rocks like Armadillidiidae vulgare, excuse me I mean pill bugs or Earth worms. Strange to me also was the timing, while Obama was on his worldwide tour. Folk brought out 200 stacks of folk out in Germany. Yep, it was a good look, but what does it do for me is my query?

Last I heard Germans don't vote up in this camp. And I aint hating, I said the same thing about McCain when he was in Israel. Not to mention, I was gonna post on his lameness today but some more brain cells started to twitch – thus the current thought crime. As I have said in maybe too many post, our economy is fucked. As well, I have recanted a number of factors and postulates as to why we are experiencing what we are. Unlike the pundits or politicians, I have offered DOABLE solutions to this economic conundrum.

But the way I see it, it will only get worse if we don't take control and create our own reality. Now I'm no leader, but I was taught that leaders do two things: create their own reality and know how to say thank you. What have they created for me thus far is a porridge of unknown proportions. I see the Dow Jones, and I see it loose and then make up some of the ground, but each time it does gain its losses, it loses another 200 to 300 points and need I remind you, that aint a good look. Dow Chemical profits dropped almost 30 percent over the past quarter, namely from what they say was due to spending 40 percent more on fuel and raw materials. Starwood Hotels, the folk that own Westin among others reported a 28% loss this past quarter and Kimberly Clark, the folk that make Kleenex and Huggies, reported a loss of 10% (due to rising energy cost as well). These are just the past quarter, I would add the last year but I don't wanna cry in public.

The problem for me, outside of the political presidential hopefully not dealing with such specifics, is that it is only happening here in this country. I mean Daiwa Securities in Japan expects a profit of anywhere from 200 to 300 million over the next quarter. Credit Suisse can manage to mogul a billion dollar plus profit for the next quarter when overall net profits dropped. The Qatar Investment Authority has just increased its stake in Barclay PLC of London by more than 6 percent or $9 billion.

Now all American Based companies aint fucking up, I mean ask Occidental Petroleum, they profits increased 63 percent the past quarter, that's right, they in oil. Now don't get upset, so I aint watch Black in America or whatever it was called. All I am saying that the America I love and know has been foul to me and mine; that it is not black or white or mauve or polka-dot. If such was the case, we would have the black and white IRS and the Yellow and red Federal government. We have neither. The America that is ours (me my, son, and daughter) is green (dollar, dollar bill yawl), regardless of the denomination. That must and should unite us all, what color is yours jones?

### 53 - Sunday, August 03, 2008
First I lied. The McCain post will be next. Any who, I know that most of us are mad as hell at these big oil companies taking all our loot and grossing big profits while at the same time they getting they corporate welfare on. And yes they are a great evil, but the greatest evil if you asked me are insurance companies. And they seem to be of late, at least since Hurricane Katrina, putting it down.

Insurance is an easy business, all they live to do is collect premiums and try they best to keep from paying out claims. With the help of the GOP, Lobbyist and judges that unlike days of old, got money invested in all kinds of stuff, they may be making civil claims and law suits for the regular man a thing of the past.

Now it is very possible that I am wrong, but times seem to have changed for the worse. After the oral argument in the Exxon Valdez case, I realized that Judges ain't judges anymore and making loot is the trump card, since Justice Samuel A. Alito Jr. had to rescue himself from hearing the case because he owned stock in Exxon. And then after the U.S. Supreme Court had a divided vote regarding the decision on Warner-Lambert Co. v. Kent, because making money for many of these judges, even on the local level is more important than administering justice. I mean they couldn't even hear a class-action lawsuit that accuses more than 50 U.S. businesses of helping South Africa's former apartheid regime because just five of the nine justices could hear the case, and six are needed for a quorum. Chief Justice John G. Roberts Jr. and Justices Breyer and Alito Jr. have holdings in some of the companies named in the suit and Justice Kennedy's son works for another, Credit Suisse Group.

The aforementioned is problematic, but what has put the icing on the cake for me is how I have Notice the company Logo for State Farm on almost every baseball field in the majors, and even during the college world series. I was used to seeing their commercials on TV, but since Katrina, seems like they have taken a scorch and burn approach. Maybe it was due to State Farm Fire & Casualty Co. being charged with a "pattern of racketeering" as a result of them manipulating engineering reports after Hurricane Katrina so they could deny policyholder claims. Since then, goo-gobs of homeowners have sued their insurers for denying their claims after the Aug. 29, 2005, storm. It was the first time an insurer was charged with violating the civil Racketeer Influenced Corrupt Organization Act, commonly known as RICO.

Since then, State farm has been on a roll, trying to get politicians, including McCain and Obama, to limit and squash the ability of folks to file civil laws suits, with due process in front of a jury. State Farm has historically spent a lot on this, but they have steeped their game up as of late. State Farm has spent has hired the Fowler White Boggs Banker firm to lobby on its behalf. Like I said, State Farm has been pushing for changes in Florida's no-fault insurance law too.

So true, the Oil companies are not folks I like too look up to, I mean I'm down with making loot, but not via extortion. But at least they have a commodity that we demand. We don't even need insurance, it's a fabrication anyway and when we need it, they fight us tooth and nail to collect. Maybe this is much to do about nothing, I mean they are the biggest crooks next to politicians to me, but at the rate that judges are recusing themselves, they may just want to give all judges stock in their company and they won't have to worry about law suites at all.

### 54 - Tuesday, August 05, 2008

Jones mane, folk here by all accounts is African – if a cat has kittens in an oven, don't make them biscuits. But my heart is here, America, American me folk. So I talk and criticized for the common good, and in good faith, something that ALL politicians don't know how to do, least since the FDR days, since now they tend to respond or react as opposed to think. So as a result, I have been very critical of these folk who are running to be this nation's commander in chief.

Now don't expect nothing sensational, nope jones, I just wanna be really real with thought. I mean I am Meek, just that and recant that Jesus was meek, but he would place the plague on your azz with the quickness.

See for me, I have held Obama to a certain level, objective without age, race or him wearing his faith on his sleeve as being a factor. Such has been waited out; maybe that's why some folks think I'm hard on Jones. I have done the same with McCain, with all of the prior, in addition to him not wearing his faith on his sleeve as canceling out.

Sometimes I think Obama just don't know what he be saying or is just unaware of what his staff write policy wise for him. But McCain, I think folk think I'm stupid. Now I won't start with his recent debacle, when Tallahassee Democrat senior writer Stephen Price on Friday was thrown out of his rally. I mean so he was the only Black reporter, and so what none of the other local press was removed, I won't touch that. And nope, I won't touch what he said when he addressed the National Urban League, when he mentioned that he would employ military's tactics in Iraq as the model for crime-fighting in American urban areas (code word for where black folk live).

No, but on disposition and policy I will. Even when it comes to economics, education and yes, even the energy policy, he maintains a banal and sublime approach to problem solving that on the one hand condemns his opponents for beliefs his fellow GOP comrades have and maintain. Like Obama on pressure in tires to save gas, when the current governor of California have; but also with respect to nuclear power; when The two Bushes and Regan held a similar stance to the democratic front runner. I mean, he tends to come across as if he can only proffer that a military solution is an answer to all things. He suggest we expand our current off shore drilling when it would be more economically feasible to be looking at the Black Sea, especially if folks like Exxon Mobil, who suspect that there may be 10 billion barrels of oil reserves in the Black Sea.

It would not even surprise me if he sided with Attorney General Michael Mukasey's call for Congress to authorize the indefinite subverting of the right of habeas corpus for anyone, even US citizens to be detained if suspected as being a terrorist, over the side of liberty. This is problematic for me since he says that he agrees and continue handling the current war as GWB does. What "Mukasey is asking is for Congress to extend the war on terror forever and that folk the president say is a terrorist can be held indefinitely without a trial.

He already wants to stay in Iraq forever, and his position on the Gaza Strip, makes me think that he may actually be one of the terrorist he himself describes. He supports Israel doing what it must to defend and protect itself, even if that includes the Israel's secret police withholding medical treatment to Palestinians in Gaza. Shin Bet Started interrogating Palestinian patients who needed to go to Israel for medical service after they set up the blockaded (which McCain supports). One would think a former POW would not support the practice of taking the sick underground to windowless rooms and using the threat of not getting medical help as a way to get them to tell on others.

And I ain't picking on McCain, for just as Obama, they don't really have an inkling of anticipation of what they are in for, but what worries me is not just his stance on the war but as I mentioned briefly, his disposition toward problem solving. From his inability to stay on point with a decision (as he did on taxes saying he is down with a higher payroll tax for Social Security, when he pledged not to raise taxes of any kind ) to his open hypocrisy via using loop holes in his own campaign finance reform law (McCain-Feingold). He does this by using folks like the Republican Governors Association (RGA), a 527 with no donation limits.

Even on topical issues regarding ethics, he has failed my test, but so has Obama. But such is the mark of desperation for his attack machine aint even started yet. And best believe the GOP hood rats will be in rare form. So another election year, and another ballot in which I will write my name in instead of either of the aforementioned.

## 55- Wednesday, August 06, 2008

So, for the record, I don't hate McCain, I just think he dying. As well don't hate Obama; he has just reducing questions to the general than toward the specific. Neither of them deal with the realities in America outside of being topical. They don't see it seems, what is going on, or how we are losing our country to outside global interest and that WE THE PEOPLE are losing out daily in this ground war. Maybe I am wrong, but from not talking about China and the steel industry while in Pennsylvania to the foreclosures in Georgia when speaking of economics, I don't hear specified answers from either. Case in point.

A British bank and investment firm has managed to buy a group of tenements buildings in East Harlem, New York. Now I have not heard either talk or mention this, not even in the topical sense of protecting America for Americans (which would be mandatory based on what I have read of both candidates' economic agendas, if they are to work.

Not only is most of Fannie Mae and Freddie Mac owned by Japan, Belgium and some selected Arab countries, Eastern and central Europe is getting in on the land grab. A London-based investment bank, has dropped about £250 million on homes in Harlem, New York. Why, because they know that gentrification in America Urban areas is big loot, a cash cow. Not just a few building I add, but a few square miles north of 100th Street. This private bank, even opened a well-staffed office in downtown Manhattan, under the name of Dawnay, Day US Real Estate Management.

We talking about more than 1000 acquisition in East Harlem in 47 buildings from the North side of Central Park from East 100th Street and East 120th Street. But I can't be mad at them, if I had Pounds, against the historical lows in the dollar.

But back to the front runners, they don't even mention this kind of stuff yet they claim to focus on and target the grass root common man. These places, like here with the foreclosures, anywhere from 40 to 50% live below the national median income annually. And how do they get folks out after they buy the properties, they raise the rent, to $1000 per square foot and evict folk. They will talk about helping Fannie Mae and Freddie Mac, as I said, but when it comes to regular folks, no mention, just the middle class. And just think, Harlem used to be a middle class community. A few years from now, middle won't be able to afford it anymore. And it seems on the surface that McCain or Obama don't even know, for I do hope and believe they care. So you can call it what you want, and suggest you label me cow, because yep, I got beef.

> *I'm talkin' big boy rides*
> *And big boy ice*
> *Let me put this big boy in yo life*

For the sagacious, even if one had the ability to afford such, in a time when oil may be approaching $200.00 a barrel and fuel efficiency in the average car is virtually no existent, the suggestion that buying such vehicles and buying jewelry to match, when it may be the result of a miner in South Africa who is prevented from seeing his wife to mine such, or a young child maimed or killed in a war to obtain such "ice", is merely a sign of selfishness traditionally reflective of western world belief orientation. There is nothing wrong with obtaining wealth, just letting such define what and who one is. This made more paramount in the following stanza:

> *Cause errbody know it ain't trickin if ya got it*
> *Ya need to never ever gotta go to yo wallet*

Even more problematic is that believing that a woman, or man doesn't have to work to provide for themselves, or support themselves, may be more harmful to the community as a whole, creating a destitute populous of folks that would rather receive handouts, feel that they should be giving things without hard work, or in encouraging the belief that I am entitled to things without work just because I want them.

In summary, although a song and not a poem or piece of well written short fiction, this song seems to represent the suggestion that value can only be in what one is worth and that anything, even a meaningful relationship or another person can be had if the price is right. Moreover it offers the belief that working and providing for oneself moot for any person, especially a woman. From this perspective, the only difference between the aforementioned works is that it is played on radios continuously and is more prevalent than books or the written word. The general translation of the song could be literally, "is u a bich or what"; specific to both men and women who abide by such beliefs. The beat is funky and the hook is catchy however, it makes one think that if Kanye West was offered by the KKK to produce a song for them called "Hang that Nigga from a tree", that many would listen to it, that it would be played on the radio incessantly, that we would say it is just a song and not find it offensive.

### 56 - Wednesday, August 13, 2008
I have heard and believe that Karma is a mother fucka. I also believe that even those that act without conscious, have one and that it eats at them when they do foul shit. That kind of makes me happy, but sad for folk like that at the same time. I mean, maybe not yet, but the foul shit GWB has implemented will come back to haunt his azz. Just like the foul shit Putin is doing in Georgia, Its gone come back to haunt his azz. Or those that take and never give, failing to count the blessings that they once had. Or the deceitful that select to not acknowledge that they be the ones who think not getting caught in a lie is the same as telling the truth.

This is also true for those that play with the hearts of other, for the fathers who do not call their sons back, or the mothers who try and figure out why their daughters do not want to have anything to do with them. For those that play with the feelings of others, who eventually cannot understand why folks feel the way they do about them. For those who expect others to keep their word but don't do so themselves and even get upset when folks don't. For them that become the lonely when they once had companionship. For them that feel empty even with all of the money they have amassed and use drinks to worship their heart, when they don't have loot to purchase gas. For those that lose their jobs, when they know the reason they lost them was their own fault.

For those that say they have no sexual desire but touch and play with themselves every night. For those that call others fools, crazy or out their names and won't speak or have a desire to speak to others until they want or need something. For those who fail classes and don't except the responsibility of studying for the classes they pay for. For those that go hungry for they are too lazy to cook. For those that believe America is a democracy when it is a republic for they do not have a desire to read the constitution. For those who claim to be godly but are the devil in personification whether it is via adultery, stealing, murder, rape or destroying that which belongs to another.

Yes this is for you. For taking for granted kindness in all respects and understanding that it returns to be the greatest pain. Especially when other use kindness in a humble attempt to reflect who they are in soul and spirit. The pain folk feel as a result of that is a consequence of their own lies, rather it regards weapons of mass destruction, promises to god, or regime change.

It is sad, but we reap what we sow. See we plant seeds, and the way we nurture them will determine the plants they foster, That's why I can't understand how folks act, or can act confused or miffed when things in their life go astray; or events occur and act as if they are amazed. For in the long time, we all get what we nurture.

Because regardless of whom we are and where we come from, we all have dirt behind our ears. I know I do, but I can admit my dirt freely, some of us cant, and we will continue to have sleepless nights, for we prefer to do battle with our conscious. Especially you Mr. President, for now since Russian President Vladimir Putin has adopted your Neo-con stance of liberating South Ossetia as we did Iraq to encourage regime change. So for you and anyone else, if the shoe fits, wear it. Not me. Like I said in the first paragraph, karma is a bitch and we reap what we sow.

## 57 - Saturday, August 16, 2008

I first found about the invasion of Georgia by Russia two Thursdays ago. I found out from reading one of my dailies, the Turkish Daily news, which is listed on my blog under news in right side bar which I read every day. Started reading it daily about 4 years ago to keep tabs on the US and Turkey and the Kurds. I wanted to write about it then but the scholar in Jones wouldn't let me for I felt there was a bigger picture with respect to history and the future. I was trying to wait to see how BO and JM would respond; I wanted to see if they had a firm understanding of the history associated with this conundrum; I desired to see if they would actually show the ability to think on this REAL BIG PROBLEM or would they just recant what their handlers told them to say. Was disappointed for the latter is all jones here got.

I know that Georgia is very important as a transit point for bringing gas and oil in from the east to the west. I also suspect that this was clearly calculated and part of the Russian foreign policy. It would not even surprise me if they gave folk who decided to break away from Georgia, the leader of South Ossetia, a fat crib and some confiscated oil loot.

But that's how folk here think. Most of Russia's wealth comes from natural gas to Europe and their gas reserves have been declining if you aint know.

But McCain and Obama don't seem to grasp the entirety of the situation. I mean, Russia is the new King of Geopolitical warfare. - A term I first read in 2005. When Russia cut off gas supplies to Ukraine in 2006-07, over pricing disputes, there were shortages throughout Europe the next day. So much so that Hungary, Austria, Slovakia and Serbia was about to implement gas rationing.

We know what oil is doing, but check this, Russia's Gazprom seems to have got the $230 per 1,000 cubic meters of gas it demanded out of Ukraine, when they got $50 the year before – can you say hustle? See Russia wants to control export routes all through that region, especially on as regarding oil and any natural resource coming from the Caspian Sea – mean them folks (and I ain't mad) want to Victor VonDoom the region and be an energy super power. And for the lame, the only pipeline which by passes Russia and takes oil from Caspian sea to rest of world is in Georgia– thus why they ganked navel ports. Now, aint much reported in America, not even of post-communist countries standing with Georgia

Ukraine, Poland, Baltic countries. Likewise, that's why I figure the two jones runni9ng for President aint got an inkling of understanding about what I'm looking at as a layman and a mother fucka who ain't as smart as them. But I will say one thang, it is obvious they aint ever read the agreement Condi and the west took to Georgia to sign. I read it and folk here aint running for president. And what I read is scary and reminds me of the Munich Agreement of 1938.

No room for international monitors, it's like it was when Hitler took over Europe. When Hitler came to power in 1933, everything he did was basically design to change the shit that hit Germany via the Treaty of Versailles. From getting Brittan to not restrict German navel expansion to getting pro-Nazi elements among the Czech Germans to want to secede from Czechoslovakia, This led Nazi aggression and a world war.

Now yawl jones running for president, Obama and McCain, I don't claim to be as smart or well-read as yawl, but I aint stupid either folk. You all ain't read the agreement, don't understand history, and are puppets regardless of party affiliation and folk here don't follow the lame. Not to mention I always wanted to be Dr. Victor Von Doom (intelligence 7 out of 7 in Marvel Universe), never no super hero. Yes, a professional criminal without a criminal record that other perceived as brilliant. So I'm down with Dr. Victor Von Doom he my Idol. Wish McCain and Obama were too, I'd be more comforted if they were.

## 58 - Tuesday, August 19, 2008

I hate to do this but I am gonna leave the pestilence of politics for a moment to dive into an area I love greatly, well two really, history and math. I was reading someone's blog yesterday and I am sorry I cannot provide the link. But in essence they were talking about the incarceration rates in NYC. I was taken back by their conclusion for although true, they were somewhat fatuous in their implications. In addition, they seemed to just be thrown out into the blogosphere for no other reason than that (my opinion) but it was a good read.

Without a firm historical presentation, the numbers in social research seem to, really often end up meaning nothing. For me, through the Euclidian structure of how I visualize thought, it is possible to decussate axioms of outcomes, both in time and practice. And I use Euclidian for it references the understanding of relationships with respect to distance (history) and angles in both planes and space. This is constant regardless of geography, region or time if space is seen as the constant. For this it says that prison and slavery are one in the same.

In the blog post, the author seemed amazed. But one should not be if a descent purview of history and thought is held in command. The Spanish government for example started out with the prohibition of having too many male slaves and in 1503, around the start of the Spanish Caribbean Empire, they enacted by philosophy and math a design that would approximate one slave for every three free white men. This was under the reign of Emperor Charles V. Other countries desired an even higher ration of white me (one African slave for every four free white men).

These actions tended to dictate not only population and how slave institutions (including prisons) functioned numerically, but also the philosophical beliefs that would maintain such disparities as evinced currently with prison populations. From David Hume, the supposedly noted philosopher to Thomas Jefferson, we can see how such transpired. Especially if you read Hume's essay *"Of National Character"* (1754) or Jefferson's *"Notes on Virginia"* (1781). Both claim the natural inferiority of the African with Jefferson even suggesting that Africans were barely above the level of thought of narration. Both said a lot more foul shit but I will not venture any further while attempting to make my point that the numbers we see are the result of historical practices and have been consistent since the days of Alexis DeToqville.

Moreover, such has been manifest by views as the previous to the extent that the belief in natural inferiority and dimness of Africans obviously would mean that education would be impossible and that a system of education, based on the liberal arts (European culture and history) would result in what I wrote in a blog post in February 2006:

If more than 50% of students drop out from high school generally, speaking, how many do you think will be coming from our schools in our neighborhoods? Take it a step farther, if 80 percent of high school drop outs end up in prison and 40 percent of all inmates are darker people, yet these people make only 13 percent of the population, what kind of educated populous will remain to do battle, represent and demand that what we put in we should get back?

There will be none for they will be enslaved, this time in prison. In actuality, I astonished myself at how simplistic the trigonometry regarding these angles connect. So in summary, this is why we see the numbers we do regarding black males in prison; this is why we should not be astonished; this is why we should not be amazed when we see more of us in prison than graduating high schools or attending college. These unfortunately are the contours of a tragedy from a Euclidian perspective, for prison is the higher education in many respects in the US for men of African descent. For with prison, they can maintain a 1 to 3, or even 1 to 4 ratio - for we outside the walls may as well be slaves too.

### 59 - Saturday, August 23, 2008

Speculative processes enables one to do many things, in particular prepare and attempt to gather understanding. In my last post, I asked a question that I have been thinking about for some time now: What happens if or when Obama loses in the general election in November. I have not really read or heard anyone discuss this or even broach this subject at all, let alone with any modicum of plausible discourse.

Seems that what is anticipated is a change. Maybe it is the intense and repetitive banter suggesting a need for change, which is true. Or maybe it is the extreme prejudice associated with the possibility of having a man of African descent take up residency on Pennsylvania Avenue. I cannot quit say but I do know that many see it as a truism albeit such has yet to take place.

Don't get me wrong, I do hope that jones wins the general election in November. However I am prepared just in case he doesn't. I cannot say the same for a large corpus of folk who take his victory as some did the Patriots over the Giants this past Super Bowl.

It may be by chance, or more so history, that he may not win. I mean historically, we have never as a people gotten this far. Even to the DNC in which a man or woman of color has been awarded the nomination for the presidency. I was taught that America granted (yes granted for freedom has only been asked for by folk like me and now taken aggressively) rights to folk like me via history and his-story in itsy bitsy baby steps. This is a big jump and complete change in discourse if jones just moves ahead of the class and claims the role of commander in chief. We see how the GOP gets down and McCain is a dirt slinging, scorch and burn, old school, chemo-drug filled mother fucking raw dawg politician.

I just really wonder how many have given true thought or discernment towards the possibility that he may lose in November to John McCain, and if he does, what happens to this country we all cherish so dearly, even with its faults. What will happen to the Democratic Party and this republic for which it stands if Obama ends up on CNN or whatever news outlet you watch and concedes to John McCain? Are you ready for that? Can you handle that? And what will happen in these streets and what will you do if he doesn't win? Cause it is real in the field.

## 60 - Monday, August 25, 2008

I made my rounds round the blogoverse and saw a lot of hoop la on the Obama VP selection. I suspect there will be a lot of hoop la when McCain select jones he wants for his running mate – I'm gone go out on a limb and say he will pick a somewhat younger white man, which won't be hard to do given McCain's age.

To be honest, Biden to me is part of the problem with Washington. Folk been up in that camp almost 4 score (I'm exaggerating). He for sure shole doesn't represent change. Then on the pic I got, he holding jones like he afraid to touch black folk like he gone get cooties or something. I would say I'm waiting for the DNC to start in Denver – but truth be told I am not ready to entertain such boredom, it's like five nights in a row of the BET hip hop awards or the Oscars all rolled up in to one. But it should be interesting.

First there is the scorn of a mean white woman with big eyes that may really come back to haunt jones. I aint mad, cause I would not have picked her back stabbing azz either. They got two nights at the convention next week so he better sick or prepare to sick ole Joe on Hill-Bill and her daughter. Has to be a first, husband, wife and child on the floor during primetime of the DNC.

I wouldn't even be surprised if she pulled the Florida and Michigan card, as I wrote a while back. But back to Biden, he sure aint no John Adams nor is he an LBJ. Biden voted for the Iraq war resolution that Obama did not vote for, talk about flip flop. And Obama picked a man who ran LAST for the presidency this year as his VP (LOL). That is if he picked him. Good old Joe even praised McCain and said Obama did not have the experience. But like I said in a comment on the last post, what is hard to put a finger on is the 20% in the middle, from Middle America, white women and blue collar workers. I figure half were for Hillary and that they may be mad as fuck she aint get picked and decided to place a revenge vote against Obama for McCain – I hope folk's aint that petty.

Then McCain, being the raw dawg GOP hood rat he is, is already trying to use this to his advantage. But you can't be mad, he is going to roll how he dogged Hill-Bill like a

Rasta would a fat azz joint to the white house. Targeting who – the blue jean, factory working white folks who voted for Hill Bill. Cause on the real, they don't connect with Barack, and connect with ChemoCain more than Obama.

But I just had to get that out. Now I can back to sleep on the sofa in my shop, it's raining now.

### 61 - Tuesday, August 26, 2008

A pulse is a rhythm, a rhythmical throbbing of arteries proffered as function of the synchronous contractions of the heart, in particular from a taxonomical perspective as palpated at the wrist or in the neck. It has also been used to describe the sentiments or views of a group (e.g. political electorate). Unfortunately, it is a reality that the pulse of America has traditionally been one built on race and racial distinctions. Since the House of Burgess to Barack Obama, this is a truism that cannot be denied. This is not to say that the majority of folks in America are racist – which they are not, but rather the material that the fabric of our country was established and founded upon. But let me table this and get to this later.

The other day I suggested that folks be prepared if Barack Obama don't win in November. I was not saying don't be optimistic, but rather realistic based on historical precedence. Sure change and a different outcome are possible, but it remains such - impossible. Unfortunately, there are those that will go in a voting both with the curtains closed and vote for McCain merely because they cannot allow themselves to vote for a person of African descent. Don't get me wrong, there is nothing wrong for voting FOR a person because of race, or gender, or ethnicity or party affiliation or because they are from your state, home town, or attended the same school you did; but there is something abhorrently despicable for not voting for a person because of such.

McCain, well I think he a dumb fk, I mean, he wants to continue the same economic policies as espoused by one George W. Bush, The failed policies of GWB at that. Such shows me he can't think nor really care about the common man. But what can you expect; this is a man with at least seven homes, and a man that can't remember how many he has. These include three beachfront cribs in Cali, condo in La Jolla, two additional condos in the same building in Coronado and a crib in Arlington, Virginia (MTV cribs here).

Then he tries to ride the POW tip like a surf board in Hawaii. Now I respect him serving his country, but as pilot 40 years ago he got shot down suggesting that he wasn't even real good at that. Jones must have had serious drain bramage seeing he doesn't even realize that Czechoslovakia is no longer a country and hasn't been a country for 37 years. Not to mention he has made reference to Iraq mixing up where the Kurds, Shiites and Sunni's actually lived.

McCain, knows he don't have to play the race card, but he will sling dirt, and play on the fears of the average jones and say that BO is just a Hollywood rock star type. So, Barack, you got to get rawdawgbuffalo with jones. And I suggest the following:

- Play on his inability to know his countries. I would suggest talking about the rate at which senility is prevalent among people his age, and ask the American Public if they would be comfortable with a man with ruptured lysosomes on his brain leading the country.
- Reverse the Rock star card. He has been on the tonight show 13 times and you only once. Who is the real Hollywood politician?
- Hammer on the fact that he has no new ideas, and that his economic plan is a carbon copy (age pun intended) of George Bush, which has failed and put us in this mess.

- Kick that fk boy Biden off the ticket and add Powell.

In essences, scare these mother fuckers mane, the voters, cause that's what he is going to do concerning you. McCain has the doric pillared stateliness of a paraplegic prior to DNR on his hospital chart.

I know you don't read my blog and I know you handlers don't even know I exist. But if you want to win, the aforementioned will help go a long way. Because anywhere from 5 to 15% of the ones who undecided, will vote for McCain because he aint black, and that really real. So question the mental capacity, compare that of one aged 71 to one 45; show how his sound bite phrases and attacks aint done jack to make our country safer. Show that a man that don't know how many houses he has aint concerned about the common man, and maybe, just maybe, you may be able to prove that one of McCain's 7 Houses is in Czechoslovakia – that is if you want to win, want my vote, and for me not to write my own name in.

## 62 - Thursday, August 28, 2008

I just want us to take a brief flicker in our busy video watching, fast food consuming and fronting for the general public days to close our eyes and honor that day jones said I HAVE A DREAM. Yep 45 years ago on this day, in Washington DC, our folks put it down. And when I say our folks, I mean our folks. Not just African Americans, but whites, Jews, male, female Asians, republic, democrats, independents families and single folk.

Strange thing is that I know the DNC rigged this day for your BO to accept his nomination. Back then, even with all of the previous marches and protest and sit ins across the South that were none violent, the media played it to the world as if the sky was falling – lord knows what's gone happen when 100 stacks plus of black folk convene in one place, in particular the nation's capital.

So they canceled major league baseball games – two of them, because the folks leaving the Washington Senator's game may get mixed up in the fray and hurt when they run into throngs of black folk. They stocked up on Plasma and closed all liquor stores for 100 thousand plus black folks were bound to riot and folks would need blood and plasma after the beat downs from twelve (police); and of course, we don't' want to sell the black folk any liquor, it will make them savage. The media also reminded women to stay inside and lock their doors, for they would less likely to be raped.

So just a few seconds, to thank folk who put it down for you to buy a 100 pair of tennis shoes, go to movies, use a single rest room regardless of color. Just a few seconds for those who read and helped their kids with their homework daily, cooked daily, and if had too, would walk to school miles and never miss a day or complain that the work or classes were too hard. For folks who sacrificed and saved for the betterment of their families and communities.

Tip your hat, and be mindful, that Mile-High Stadium holds 75K, and that it is open air, and that my favorite Rifle is the SKS (See cover of my book), and that it has a 3 mile range, and fires the 7.62.

I hope all are safe out that camp. So I say b safe BO outside ion Denver and a few seconds to our folk for these 45 years since, and take that with you.

## 63 - Saturday, August 30, 2008

I want to say the same week I wrote that Barack Obama should select Collin Powell for VP (back in April); I wrote that McCain should Pick Sarah Palin. But I did not publish it. When I suggested to folk that Obama may lose in November, they hated and said that I was not optimistic, and that such was fatuous. All I was saying was be practical, and except probability and chance as what it is. I added that I don't expect to get a flat, but I do have a spare.

I just figured that black folks were just so excited that we got happy go lucky and just knew his victory would be a certainty in November. Not to mention that we were not being very pragmatic. Then after I heard Jones speech, I was even more troubled when I knew that it did little in attempting to persuade the 20% I have been referencing in the last few essays to vote for him. So I lied, but I want to reinforce what I said about this 20 percent before. These folk let me tell you. They focus on one point as being more important than all other issues, maybe abortion or gay rights. They feel that Hillary makes or made a better speech. They feel that Barack is a speech only person. They feel that because a man gets his plane shot down that it makes him more knowledgeable on war or issues of war. They feel that his words are merely poetic rhetoric and that he is just a great speaker. They hear him and think he is just going to spend more money and that he is anti-rich. They will say they will write in Mitt Romney or Bob Barr (which benefits Barack). Or that they hear promises, and don't hear sound fiscal ideas behind the words. This makes the Palin choice both entertaining and interesting.

Albeit the choice of Palin is reckless. He say we need to get to know slim but McCain only met her just once himself. But I ain't mad and even like a woman that hunt and fish. Historically as we know, married women tend to vote conservative and she will give McCain what he has been missing – enthusiasm. She teaches creationism in Alaska school and endorsed Pat Buchanan in 2000. So it was a choice made on getting elected, not experience, although some will say she has a good record, all that 2 years can proffer. She will give him a bump with 2nd amendment advocates because gun owners don't have no love for McCain and she may even provide some vigor to what was his lethargic base. Then her son is about to head off to the battle front shortly and that's a good look for any candidate these days.

She will be expected to assume the presidency if McCain wins; a man that has had cancer four times. And again, these two folk barely know each other – can you say senile. To me it's basically like picking Tom Cruise because he can get box office draw – not a very talented actor at all. Stated simply, she is a woman, a white woman, supporter of gun rights and anti-abortion. Please show your folk here you can think, leave the emotion alone, it don't count in the voting booth, be objective and pragmatic – act like you can think. Because you all (the front runners) scaring the fuck out of jones here mane.

### 64 - Wednesday, September 03, 2008
So this is for you, the GOP. True I hate on the Democrats too, but this is your day. I guess that all you say is for the social conservatives, which means it aint for me, since I am Memphis Mac. But I hate being played like a step child. You say "hope is a false promise", but if such is the case, then it tells me you do not have faith or abide by such. Meaning that hope and faith from your point of order is self-serving. I also want to add that folk here tired of sound bites, albeit you say that Barack Obama is a sound bite fiend. I agree. But problem is you all are too – please show me a distinction. You say John McCain is a leader, and that we need a leader like John McCain. My problem is that I don't follow nobody, let alone a politician, that is supposed to serve me. I figure Jones supposed to follow me. That's what is wrong with this system in the first place. So don't get it twisted, I don't follow nobody folk, I just don't get down like that abiding by the 14th amendment as I do.

But it is nice to see McCain go after the black vote; what better way to do such than with a grand momma in her 40's. So much for abstinence only education and the scary thing is when you see it don't work, you still prop it up like cold fusion. Not to mention you all sound like democrats. You complain and say Obama gone have all these programs to spend our loot, but yet you tell me you gone build all these nuclear reactors like it ain't costing me jack. Where the money coming from, tell me that. Oh my mistake, you don't even acknowledge deflation as a threat to our economy – and I don't make 5 million a year folk, seeing that's your standard of being poor. And don't be giving jones here no incentive for having health insurance, as much money as I have spent in Iraq, I should have paid for it by now, although I know taking care of Iraqi's is more important than me in terms of dollars. Fuck them, I ain't got no problem with them, but I do with them getting more from my tax dollars than I do. Besides, when they or if they come up in this camp me and mine gone handles ours, even on your behalf even though I don't support you – but that's how Americans get down.

I won't touch on Palin, although she does remind me of that Indo-G song "when I die, die, don't you cry, cry remembers me, Palin, Palin." So take that, I had to get it off of my chest, I mean I'm down with country first, but it sound like a disinfectant or air freshener, and I prefer Fabuloso. And true, McCain maybe the most prepared and most experience, but don't forget - most likely to die in office. And please no more images of Republicans dancing off beat on CSPAN.

### 65 - Saturday, September 06, 2008
I guess John McCain and his running mate are so busy stealing Barack Obama's mantra of change; and that Obama is so busy trying to show a segment of white folk he aint no follower of liberation theology, that North Korea done fail off the map. Wish they both could be forward thinking but I guess that is like asking George Bush to like black folk or

McCain to mention slave ships in those welcome to the shores of America.

I take it both of them are so caught up in their mirrors looking at themselves that they ain't even though or even remember that country over there yonder, North Korea. I was being the slimy cat I can be when it comes to economics and politics and find out all kind of stuff. For some reason or another, few have made reference to the recent announcement that Pyongyang has started working to restore its nuclear facilities – specifically the Yongbyon nuclear plant. But you know how we do, we look the other way and say some shit like North Korea is only moving equipment out of storage. How could this be when they said a few weeks ago that last week that they had stopped dismantling the Yongbyon nuclear reactor?

At least Obama wants to meet with these fools, McCain old azz don't even want to talk, and he a leader. Shit, Crips and bloods can meet, I expect my President or any jones who desires to be my president to have the balls to meet anyone – I would. If my penchant was to put my country and protect my folk first.

I know both of them are in opposition to President's Bush modified approach – but they ain't being asked about it thoroughly on the stump. I just wonder how McCain can say we down with nuclear power development but yet other countries can't be. Why we got to be the only ones in the world that want to reduce a dependency on foreign oil? So what they got the North Korea's declaration of its nuclear program, we need to be consistent in our foreign policy and keep NK on point.

All I'm saying folk, is I may be just a cat from Memphis, but that don't mean I can't think. I thought you cats were battling for my vote. But seems to me both want me to write my own name in, and I ain't running for office.

109

## 66 - Sunday, September 14, 2008

Maybe it's just me, but it seems as if all politics has gotten off target. Especially when I look at the Obama campaign. The way I see it there are about 50 days left to the super bowl. He needs to be in the tunnel, screaming and ready to take the field. But for some reason he is slacking in his macking, he aint got his game face on, and unfortunately, he has gotten distracted and taken the bait McCain put in front of him. He has been more focused on Sara Palin, Lipstick, Pigs and waffles than on his own play book.

He even act as if he doesn't see that that is exactly what the opposition desires, for they ain't talked about nothing of substance with any semblance of astuteness to this day. Shit, we, the general public know more about lil momma than John McCain. Now I'm not taking sides but I must give my folk an informed heads up on what may be required.

First, fuck talking about McCain trying to say he for change. Let folk talk, he will eventually put a foot in his mouth. Instead, talk about his record, being a friend of big business; make him one of them, saying he is not the common man like George W. Bush. The best way to do this is to associate it directly to the economy, specifically the failing housing market. How can a man with more than five houses know what such an experience is like? Make sure that you connect him to this in tangible and political terms. Ask where has he been for the past two plus decades when all these problems started? Why historically, has he been against regulation of the Securities Exchange Commission and in support of the hideous accounting practices that hide pertinent information to the common investor (like George Bush)? Point out that he believes the market is self-correcting, but query as to how can such be, if the problem we see in housing is due to folks on Wall Street paying people to rate securities as being solid or good when they are not (like George Bush)?

They take unprecedented action to save the big financial institutions like the investment bank Bear Stearns but nothing for the common man. Particularly Securities and Exchange Commission (SEC) Chairman Christopher Cox. One of the men McCain was considering as a VP running mate. Make special note of how the Senate Banking Committee asked Cox if legislation or more resources would be needed to prevent future problems such as these from occurring, even suggesting that the credit rating institutions, who are paid by wall street to rate securities (MBS's), have a inherit conflict of interest, and that he said no, and Fannie Mae and Freddie Mac had to be bailed out like Bear Stearns. Can you say corporate welfare? This is not the common man. No wonder China owns 374 billion of US debt in the form of mortgage loans/debt

True, McCain got a little game, or else you would not have let Jones campaign buy the rights to the top search engines on key election terms. I'm telling you, ignore the mundane and attack your opponent weakness. His ability to think and side against the common man. I'd even bring up that he was a POW, and that he needs to release to the public that he has been screened for Post-Traumatic Stress Disorder, for no one with such should be answering that red phone at 3am. Now get busy folk, get your game face on and stop slacking in your macking. Just my two cents, that is if you want to win, and I got more too.

### 67 - Wednesday, September 24, 2008

I will be going on a brief hiatus from politics and the economy, or at least I think I am and that I will try my best. But seeing that it is very improbably that jones here will serve as some ones campaign advisor, better yet, the chief of staff; or will never ever be the president up in this camp, I got a few things I want to say about what I want to hear from Obama and McCain and Nader, and McKinney, and Baldwin and

Barr. So please preface the following statements with mother fuca please:

- Talk about the national debt
- Talk about prosecuting the folk on Wall Street
- Talk about eliminating penalties associated with capital gains, if one desires to use money from 401Ks or stocks that they liquidate from their portfolios if they have hardship or use the cash to start a business
- Talk about regular jones the same way you talk about corporate jones
- Talk about how we lose so much human capital via prison and the prison industrial complex and how you would treat drug use as a health issue and not a crime.
- Talk about helping to engender small business growth and reinvigorating the manufacturing sector.
- Talk about how you will increase the value of the dollar
- Talk about screening for the best teachers and paying them as if they are the best and connect education to the collective economic well-being of America
- Talk about freezing the rise in pay for senators and congressmen and the need for them not to give themselves a pay raise every 6 months
- Talk about why the lower and middle class folks can't and don't have good paying jobs or afford homes and what you plan to do to fix that.

As you may have noticed I have not posted an essay in more than a month, not that I was not writing or thinking but because I lost my grandmother a few days before Thanksgiving and my aunt, my mother's eldest sister, who lived with my granny a few days before Christmas – add that to trying to keep my business opened, I have been extremely occupied. However this week, while, at a restaurant, I was able to see the news coverage regarding Haiti. I also saw some of the coverage while over my daughters Godparent's house.

Now it is a very sad conundrum, the aftermath of the Earthquake. Seeing people dead in the streets, maimed, injured and dying is enough to make one's flesh crawl. It was devastation that I could not imagine. Now with that said, I don't want folks to take this the wrong way albeit I don't care – but what good is relief and news coverage if it only parades folks for the purpose of individual attention and ratings. What little I saw gave me this opinion and this as a man who has worked in places all over Africa stopping infectious disease pandemics in small rural communities. When I see news folk broadcasting, all I can think is that they may be sorry but really don't care and that they really acting, just like the major relief groups as well. Unfortunately, our government places more importance on getting military troops on the ground than physicians. And then there are the media pundits.

They ask questions as if the folk in Haiti could have dealt with this not recalling that the last Earthquake to occur was some 200 years ago. Then they stand over folks and as opposed to presenting news they present commentary. Figure if they really cared they would be sleeping in the fields with the folk they covering instead of hotels, and being out removing rubble instead of taking pictures and showing make-believe I care faces. Then there is the issue of not knowing history. Reporters never speak of how Woodrow Wilson and the US occupied Haiti in 1915, or how we basically killed folk on site, or how Bill Clinton continued the same progressive political approach of Woodrow Wilson. And yep, I'm not in support of progressives for around the world they feel that folks can't solve their own problems and prefer to interfere and mess things up and ex post facto blame the targets. We forget that the French and even we who did not even recognize them as a sovereign nation on until 1862 made Haiti poor. We neglected them then for years and now we blame them and don't even see how we made them or accept that we made them one of the four poorest nations on the globe. And I won't even mention all this talk about orphans and having folks in America on TV looking sad because they can't get the kid they wanted to adopt – when these same folks don't even want to adopt black kids in their own backyard.

This is why I don't watch TV news – they will pass anything over as objective information and we are too ignorant to see that what is presented is neither objective nor information but rather conjecture empty of historic perspective. Cut your TV folks, they making you make yourselves slaves. We should see that there is enough research on Earthquakes and their impact historically to act as if this is a new thing and we have to study to help folk on the ground – humbug. I wonder what else is really going on in the world, because it isn't being covered given eleventy-seven news reporters are all occupied with Haiti.

### 69 - Monday, February 15, 2010
Ok I'm back, sorry have a lot on my plate but not enough to prevent a simple jactitation on the current President of the United States and his cronies. Now I know we all know this is Black history month, a month in which we should I figure be trying to focus on education or even bringing to the fore, past wrongs in an attempt to correct them.

If you did not know, this is the 100-year anniversary of the legendary Jack Johnson and James Jeffries fight, which occurred during the summer of 1910. Born in Galveston, Texas in 1878 as Arthur John Johnson, he was the first African man to win the heavyweight boxing championship of the world. His life was one of hardship. His family lost all they owned in the great Hurricane of 1900 and he was arrested in Texas for boxing since it was against the law and considered a blood sport. Before becoming Champion of the world, Jim Jeffries refused to fight him because he was black. However Johnson went to Australia and defeated Tommy Burns to win the title in 1908, which forced Jeffries to fight him if he desired the title. After Johnson put the smack down on Jeffries (the first great white hope), folk lost their minds. There were race riots; the Texas state legislature even banned the showing of films of his victory. The only thing that could be employed to "handle" Johnson were Federal laws – mainly the Mann Act, of which he was charged for transporting white women across state lines for "immoral purposes" – a charge that was completely false. The original name of the Mann Act was the "White Slave Traffic Act". In 1913, he was imprisoned, as were many other African men to follow including Chuck Berry.

Sen. John McCain and House Rep. Peter King last year pushed a resolution through the Senate and House of asking for President Obama to pardon Johnson. However, Obama's head of the Justice Department, Eric Holder, and staff said no, suggesting they do not "traditionally" pardon dead folk compared to people "who can truly benefit" from a pardon. Truth is that Bill Clinton pardoned Henry O. Flipper, the first black graduate of the U.S. Military Academy at West Point in 1999, who was wrongly accused of embezzlement and G.W. Bush pardoned Charlie Winters in 2008 for illegally selling planes to Israel during the Arab-Israeli war in 1948.

Strange to me that Obama is always talking about change, but his actions seem to continue the problematic approaches to politics that we have seen historically by folks trapped inside the beltway. So Mr. President, Pardon Jack Johnson, because, for some strange reason, I thought you ran on a mantra of change, not the same ole same old.

### 70 - Tuesday, February 23, 2010

One of the benefits of being the President of the United States of America, if time is on your side is stacking the United States Supreme Court. Obama has made one move with a Latino woman but he may have the chance to put another one on giving John Paul Stevens, the senior Associate Justice of the Supreme Court of the United States is 90 years of age. He joined the Supreme Court in 1975 and may not have that many years to live.

My concern is that I think Obama will put a man in office that scares the crap out of me - Cass Sunstein. Obama has been linked very closely to Sunstein since their faculty days at the University of Chicago law school and has appointed him to direct the White House Office of Management and Budget's Office of Information and Regulatory Affairs (OIRA), His job is to mainly to put in place regulations to protect health, safety and the environment but history has shown us otherwise, but that is beside the point.

He is a major proponent of cost-benefit analysis as the basis for assessing regulations, even though mathematically it is not precise and can be easily manipulated to support whatever policy is retro chic. For example, it was he who used such an approach to developing his "senior discount" method for undervaluing the lives of seniors with respect to health care. He has even asked that popular or partisan websites to be FORCED to carry links to opposing viewpoints; something I will never do, could you imagine neo-Nazis and white supremacist posting on my blog? Taking this farther, he even wants mandatory "electronic sidewalks" for cyberville. He would like a "notice and take down" law that would mandate bloggers and service providers to "take down falsehoods upon notice," even if they are made by commenter's.

In a 2008 Harvard Law paper called "*Conspiracy theories*" Sunstein suggested that the government should ban conspiracy theorizing asserting to me that he does not desire for individuals to think independently or ask questions if it is against the body politic of who is in control of the government.

His position is that unrestrained individual choice if not controlled or regulated by the government is dangerous and must balance in the interests of "citizenship" and "democracy." He stated that "a system of limitless individual choices, with respect to communications, is not necessarily in the interest of citizenship and self-government. Democratic efforts to reduce the resulting problems ought not to be rejected in freedom's name." Unlike the most of us, he sees the Internet as dangerous and that the Internet is destroying the ability for the masses to have shared social experiences.

He also is against using what is called the "precautionary principle" as a basis for regulating environmental, which he would like to give the "benefit of the doubt," over possible health and safety concerns of the public. If you have read Sunstein's new book, "*On Rumors: How Falsehoods Spread, Why We Believe Them, What Can Be Done*,"

He is concerned that in the future," people's beliefs" will be are a "product of social networks working as echo chambers in which false rumors spread like wildfire."

Sunstein suggest that the current libel standard - which requires proving "actual malice," even if one blogger or newspaper, that we should even be held responsible even for what people who comment on or blog say, this is true even for web service providers.

117

Cass Sunstein is a scary mother shut your mouth and I don't believe that many folk even know or cares are even up on folk, his writings, his papers, his belief or his policies. If you are not, then you need to be – he is the antithesis of liberty in word, belief and practice. Although he claims to be a progressive, he is more of a regressive to me. So take my advice and don't be surprised if he is the person Obama select to take the place of John Paul Stevens on the United States Supreme Court. There will be a real mark of the beast on America.

### 71 - Monday, April 05, 2010

It is only fitting that on this day we revisit history and not just any history, but that which empowered one Martin Luther King Jr., to embark on the continuation of the works, ideas and beliefs of freedom and liberty. Yes freedom and liberty for even with knowledge of King, Frantz Fanon, and Thomas Jefferson, such knowledge is lost on the hearts and minds of others. I say this because I have come to the empirical conclusion that many folks of my ethnic persuasion have accepted that we are free or even worse – think we are free. Truth is that many cannot tell the difference nor explain what separates liberty from freedom, or a right from a privilege.

For me, the concepts all start with the fundamental understanding of sovereignty – a construct imbued in us not from or by any man but rather a Supreme Being or higher power. Sovereignty means supreme or highest in power. To be sovereign means to be independent of, and unlimited by, any other; possessing, or entitled to, original authority or jurisdiction. This is what liberty and freedom are based on in these United States of America with respect to the un-alienable rights men documented in the constitution.

I say this because a sovereign individual is self-reliant and does not need anyone (even government) to provide for him, protect him from himself nor tell him what to do. To be sovereign means to be responsible for one's own actions, to be financial independent and free from unnecessary government interference – basically living the life he desires. The problem again is that many do not understand these concepts or how mandates are in direct opposition from the aforementioned concepts.

Recently Obama passed a health care reform bill that mandates folks buy health insurance, similar in the vein that we are mandated to purchase auto insurance and or wear seat belts (if your state demands such by law). Truth is some states do not and that there were times that it was not required to buy auto insurance or wear seatbelts. Many may be too young to remember such, but it is true. When I mentioned my problem with this to a friend, he told me that he was glad such was mandated because driving is not a right but rather a privilege. I said that anything one can do, create or think of is legal and provided to me by that greater than me and not a man. Also added that by their logic, reading and learning is a privilege also for that is how slave masters saw it – that they could decide for you as government entities do now. I also added that also though it was unnecessary for marriage license, gun permits and driver's license. Again he disagreed. So I reminded him of why we have both.

There was a time when there was no such thing as either, that is until or near the end of slavery. Historically, all the states outlawed the marriage of blacks and whites. Not until the mid-1800s did some states allow such but in order to do so, they were mandated to receive a license from the state (had to get permission to do an act which without such permission would have been illegal). *Black's Law Dictionary* notes historically that a marriage license is defined as, "A license or permission granted by public authority to persons who intend to intermarry." "Intermarry" is defined in Black's Law Dictionary as, "Miscegenation; mixed or interracial marriages." Up until this period there was no such thing and now states all use them, as a way to make money for God requires no such permit.

The same is true with respect to Gun permits. Throughout much of American history, gun control was used as a method for keeping blacks in check due to the racial fears of whites. Racist arms laws were on the books before the US was established. The French Black Code (required Louisiana colonists to stop "any black carrying any potential weapon, such as a cane)." If a black refused to stop on demand and was on horseback, the colonist was authorized to "shoot to kill." Even before that the sixteenth century the colony of New Spain, prohibited all blacks, free and slave, from carrying arms. Mississippi went further and prohibited any ownership of a dog by a black person. Such restrictions increased dramatically after Nat Turner's Rebellion in 1831. Virginia's response to Turner's Rebellion prohibited free blacks "to keep or carry any firelock of any kind, any military weapon, or any powder or lead". Simply, America has a fear of armed blacks based on the collective unconscious of what many made the Africans in America experience. Even at the end of slavery nothing was instituted to eliminate or change racist gun control laws. Blacks even needed to obtain a license before carrying or owning a gun or knife when such was not required for whites. Even today the same practices based on race via mandates stem from what we saw in the years of slavery. From public housing residents being singled out for gun bans to so-called "Gun sweeps" by police in "high crime" neighborhoods.

All I am trying to say that we speak and accept these mandates by the government and they are often accepted under the guise of privilege as opposed to a right. We do not value freedom or liberty as much as we say or we would have continued the struggle that our fore parents lead. It seems again as we think we are free, or think we have made or think we have overcome, but the truth is we accept without question. Accepting mandates as such makes us slaves, obviates us from individual responsibility and takes away our enumerated rights stated in the constitution. It is not rocket science – if we are not sovereign, we have no liberty, if we have no liberty we have no freedom if we have no freedom we have no rights – all that is left is privilege, which by definition can be given and/or taken away at any time.

## 72 - Monday, April 26, 2010

If you are an avid reader, you may be well aware of two of the finest works of science fiction written over the past 100 years: Aldous Huxley's *A Brave New World* and George Orwell's *1984*. In *A Brave New World*, Huxley attempts to warn us of a future plagued with interest supportive of scientific utopianism. A world in which, people are just victims of propaganda to be manipulated. In *1984*, George Orwell describes a petrifying dangers that man, in search of a Utopia may create via government in order to have an orderly society, but at the expense of the freedom of the people. In the book "Big brother" is always watching, "Ignorance is strength" and "freedom is slavery."

Yesterday, the U.S. Library of Congress said it would start saving and archiving all worlds' tweets from around the world due to a new partnership with Twitter. Each public tweet from 2006, when the first began to date will be archived. This means that all information that is on the public timeline, from Twitpic, to your location, to any link will be recorded for all of history for anyone to search and study.

This just displays how significant view the Internet is in this digital age. After six months, all public tweets will be made available to the Library of Congress. It has been estimated that between 50 to 60 million of tweets are published each day. Biz Stone, one of the founders of the microblogging service wrote "...there are some specifics regarding this arrangement. Only after a six-month delay can the

Tweets will be used for internal library use, for non-commercial research, public display by the library itself, and preservation."

So be leery of what you send out in your limited 140-character space, for if you plan to run for congress or any political office, your tweets will be available for you opponents to use anyway fit.

### 73 - Tuesday, May 04, 2010

The massive oil slick in the Gulf of Mexico is finally reaching the shores of the Gulf Coast, in what many have called the worst environmental disaster since the 1989 Exxon Valdez spill in Alaska. Not only does it have the potential to threaten hundreds of species of fish, birds and other wildlife in the area, but, more importantly, the livelihood of many who make a living fishing in the nation's richest seafood region.

More than 200,000 gallons of oil a day have been spewing into the ocean since British Petroleum's Deep-water Horizon oil rig exploded and sank off the Louisiana coast last week. Homeland Security Secretary Janet Napolitano stated that BP is "the responsible party" according to U.S. law and is "required to fund the cost of cleanup operations." In fact, in a letter sent last year to the Department of the Interior, the oil giant objected to what it described as "extensive, prescriptive regulations" proposed for more rigorous safety standards stating. "We believe [the] industry's current safety and environmental statistics demonstrate that the voluntary programs ... continue to be very successful."

Last year, BP made more than 40 billion in profits yet paid no taxes in the United States.

This oil spill could not have come at a more significant time given that just a few weeks ago President Obama asked Congress to lift a drilling ban in the eastern Gulf of Mexico, 125 miles from Florida beaches and called for new offshore drilling in the Atlantic Ocean from Delaware to central Florida.

President Barack Obama has pledged "every single available resource" to deal with the situation and called the leak a "spill of national significance,"

The real threat is to thousands of independent African American and small businesses in the region that make a living via fishing and tourism. If there is a significant reduction in the oyster, shrimp and fish populations, which has been in decline anyway over the past decade, it may signal an end to the livelihoods of many.

In Louisiana for example, African-Americans own 12 percent of all businesses with coastal cities like Baton Rouge having 17 percent black-owned business, most in the fishing and tourism industries. The same can be said of Mobile, Ala., where 14.8 percent of businesses are black-owned compared to 9 percent for the state of Alabama. If this problem is not under control soon, many families' owned and small African American businesses in the Gulf region may not survive.

## 74 - Monday, August 16, 2010

A recent report in The Washington Post has revealed that the Obama administration is seeking to make it easier for the FBI to collect information on the personal Internet activities of American citizens without the requirement of a search warrant.

The change, if implemented, would give the executive branch and the FBI increased powers by forcing companies to provide upon request, the records of any individual's Internet activity without being required to obtain a court order.

According to the Post, the Obama administration will be able to provide information to the FBI if they feel it is important and pertinent to a "terrorism or intelligence investigation." Merely by inserting the words "electronic communication transactional records" to a list of materials that current laws state that the FBI may request without the approval of a judge. This includes personal user Internet web browser activity and the addresses to which an individual sends e-mail. More important is that the request would be secretly obtained and withheld from the individual user.

Unknown too many is that according to government sources, many Internet and e-mail services already provide the government with such data. During his campaign, Obama ran on many issues, including enhancing individual civil liberties. However, this effort may lead to an erosion of individual rights and privacy. In 2007, a published report by the Inspector General's office revealed that the FBI might have incurred many violations in requesting such data — including the solicitation of information without having an approved investigation to justify the request.

Warrantless surveillance programs are unconstitutional, yet the current administration, following where former President George W. Bush left off, argues that such information is the same or equal to telephone toll billing records, which the FBI can obtain without court authorization. This means that finding out who a person sends e-mail to or a Facebook friend request is the same as a telephone call.

It would seem as a constitutional law scholar, Obama would understand that the First Amendment protects the personal association information of a citizen.

The question is how this might impact future government legislation. On March 4, 2010, the "Enemy Belligerent Interrogation, Detention, and Prosecution Act of 2010" was introduced by John McCain. This bill, if passed, would eliminate several constitutional protections allowing the government to arbitrarily pick up Americans on mere suspicion — with no probable cause. Not to mention, in May of this year, the president gave a speech in which he asked Congress to pass legislation to give the president, power to detain any person in the U.S. that the government deems a "combatant" or likely to engage in a violent act in the future.

How far does the government plan to go invade the private lives of its citizens under the guise of national security? We will have to wait and see, for it seems to reflect what Huxley predicted would happen in a totalitarian society in his book *Brave New World*.

## 75- Friday, August 20, 2010

It is not hard to find hard-core criticism floating through the air like pollen regarding our nation's first African-American president. Some of which is deserved, most of which is not and is simply, colloquially speaking, hating. The overwhelming corpus of which comes from Republicans on the far and middle right.

This is more than obvious — so obvious, in fact, that many on the right have manifested behaviors reflective of the tenets espoused by Freud when he discussed defense mechanisms.

From extreme projection (in which a person lacks consciousness of their own thoughts and ascribes those unconscious thoughts to others) to denial (refusal to accept external reality because it is too threatening), everything this segment of the political spectrum says is targeted towards Obama. Now some would say it is politics, as usual, but I disagree with that assertion.

Recently, right-wing radio talk-show host Laura Ingraham stated that first lady Michelle Obama's Whitehouse garden was a "left-wing plot."

Glenn Beck, in a similar vein, speaking about the outfit the first lady wore to her visit to the Gulf, described it as an "outrage."

It is difficult to empirically understand such comments since they have nothing to do with the real political issues at hand. It can simply be reduced to behavioral neuro-

125

ses that are rooted in America's steep tradition of racial vili-
fication, which traditionally manifests in personal attacks and
demonization.

The reality is that the GOP is out of ideas, and rather
than thinking about solving the nation's problems, would rather stoke over-the-top paranoia, which if history is any indication, often results in violence. Just ask anyone who had
dogs released on them, water from a fire hose sprayed on
them, or anyone with a family member hung from a tree or
dragged from a truck.

Insanity is a serious and debilitating condition that
disrupts one's capacity to function within the legal limits of
society, which results in both a deranged mind and (too)
many times, a tragic outcome.

## 76 - Tuesday, August 31, 2010

Politics can be reduced to a game of he said she said with the
gender specific pronouns being replaced by the nouns Democrats and Republicans. This is certainly clear with the debate
on unemployment. Both parties have been successful at taking the focus away from the real issue, which is unemployment, choosing instead to focus on the fake issue — extension of benefits for the unemployed.

Neither side of the aisle has addressed unemployment
outside of name calling and bickering. The real question,
which neither the Republicans nor the Obama administration
is asking, is where do 8.4 million jobs that were lost come
from and what is required to be done for the younger generation entering the job market to also have jobs?

The fact is that no program can make up for the loss
of that many jobs, so America will have to get accustomed to
double-digit unemployment. Although many accept the government's projected figure of around 10 percent for unemployment, I have calculated it to be more like 25 for the general population. Which means if it is that high for the general

population, the 16 percent propounded to represent the unemployment rate for African Americans is really closer to 35 percent.

The way unemployment figures are calculated currently, military, college students, part-time workers, and seniors are not included in the statistics. As it stands, the economic downturn has hit the African American community harder than any other group. This was also true during the Great Depression when we also were impacted disproportionately.

New data shows that the median duration of unemployment is higher today than any time in U.S. history and is really are more than twice as high today as any time in the last 50 years. The reason is a function of two main components: the loss of jobs to cheap labor abroad and the impact of technology on society.

Many jobs over the last 50 years have been eliminated due to technology. No longer are men required to dig ditches, package or can food items or man gas stations. No longer do we focus on creating and manufacturing as in past decades but rather bartering our services. Obama's solution as a function of the observed 1.5 dip recession is to institute a large-scale national jobs program that would have the government pay these wages directly. The Republicans, on the other hand, have no specific policy directive. Both of these approaches are equally ineffective and miss the problem completely.

The new American job market will be one filled with temporary hiring and part-time employment. Neither the Democrats nor the Republicans can institute any policy to change the future landscape of the American job market because of the impact that technological advancement plays in increasing the ranks of the unemployed. I said it before and I will say it again, there is no such thing as a jobless recovery.

## 77 - Sunday, September 12, 2010

It is difficult for me to understand why politicians and our civilian population in America are so distracted and seem to display the inability to see through the shady penumbra of what is promulgated both in the media and inside the beltway.

I have been told by the aforementioned that we as Americans should be worried about what a fringe right wing psychopathic zealot in Florida plans to do on this upcoming anniversary of 9/11. I cannot see how this man with the following somewhere around the size of a professional football team is of any significance.

The more it is discussed the more I am unable to figure out why it is newsworthy unless there is some unseen or unspoken back room motive behind it. The truth is that I could care less as to what this man does as well as other Muslim fundamental extremist. So what really can this idiot do to put us at risk after all that we have done in Iraq, Pakistan and Afghanistan already?

I obviously have a different purview than Secretary Clinton and General Petraeus. It is lucid that they separate what our military and political actions are and have been in the past. From our documented torture of detainees, targeted assassination and drone strikes, our incessant occupation of Muslim countries, tens of thousands of civilian casualties and the recent report of US soldiers killing Afghan civilians for fun and collect their fingers as trophies.

How quickly we forget or worse do not see, that we are doing exactly what extremist desire for us to do. To hate and openly discriminate, to retract the freedoms we take for granted from others. I am an American and although and African American, I know there is much more that can be done to make this country support me as the mainstream. However, still, I am not afraid

I just don't see how this is less of a provocation that a confederate throwback preacher oral plan to burn Qurans. We as Americans are so used at deflecting blame and impetus to others that we can't even own up to our own shit. Personally, I say fuck it, fuck what the extremist think here and abroad. But I do see that America has become sissified, for saying such is truly a lost art.

## 78 - Tuesday, September 14, 2010

Newt - by definition any of various small amphibious salamanders with amphibian in the latter sense meaning having two natures. For Newt Gingrich, this means slimy and full is do-do. In an interview with the National Review Online, speaking of Obama-Gingrich said, "This is a person who is fundamentally out of touch with how the world works, who happened to have played a wonderful con, as a result of which he is now president."

The supposedly astute scholar of history went even further saying, "What if [Obama] is so outside our comprehension, that only if you understand Kenyan, anti-colonial behavior, can you begin to piece together [his actions]?" He continued his bazaar and inaccurate proposition on Fox News Sunday, criticizing the president's economic policy saying, "The thing that the president doesn't understand and the thing that Keynesian economics gets wrong is real simple: Do you want people to have enough money to invest in creating jobs? If they have a surplus of income so they can create jobs, that's somehow bad and the president wants to take away the income. That means he's leaving them with no money to create jobs."

He admitted that his thought was influenced by an article written by Dinesh D'Souza for Forbes Magazine in which D'Souza extended the psychotic paranoia of the Tea Party and so-called birthers saying "the U.S. is being ruled according to the dreams of a Luo tribesman of the 1950s."

This being a specific reference to Obama's father. He connected this to Obama by writing "Here is a man who spent his formative years--the first 17 years of his life--off the American mainland, in Hawaii, Indonesia, and Pakistan, with multiple subsequent journeys to Africa." As if to say being from Hawaii is less valuable than being born on mainland USA or being a descendant of Africa is even worse.

Both Gingrich's and D'Souza's assertions are sentiments only a country built on racism could support. It is unlikely that such would be said of a man who was the president whose father was born in Ireland or any other European Nation. I would even venture to say that neither man has ever lived in Africa nor are even astute on the history of colonialism and it impacts on the political psyche of Africans around the world. We are always reminded of the impact of colonialism and imperialism in for of both slavery and the stealing of natural resources that Europe and the West continue until this day.

The Luo comprise around 12% of Kenya's population, making it the 3rd largest ethnic group after the Kikuyu and the Luhya. If Gingrich or D'Souza had any remote understanding of African culture or history they would see the absurdity of their position since the Luo were not particularly troubled by the arrival of the white Europeans and settlers, did not have their land taken like the Kikuyu and the Luhya and were not particularly involved in the Mau Mau rebellion. What they did was help to create an independent Kenya through politics as opposed to violence. Unlike the radical colonialist who formed this nation, we live in here - America. If I am not mistaken, Jefferson, Washington, Madison, Franklin and Hamilton all were self-described anti-colonist.

Gingrich and D'Souza's are what is wrong with the Republican Party and they wonder why they are seen as being extremist zealots with distinct phobias against anything other than white Anglo-Saxon Protestants. If this is all the

130

GOP has to offer, and their thought is a continues to be a hodgepodge of flippant inaccuracies and attempts to divide instead of amalgamate, then I say GOD save America and any person in America who is not white.

## 79 - Thursday, September 16, 2010

Since Martin Luther King Jr.'s assassination, African Americans without question have voted hook, line, and sinker for the Democratic Party. As a consequence of this blind allegiance, we often fail to see the similarities of Democrats and Republicans — namely that regardless of race and gender, they all — for lack of a better term — are crooks and place themselves and their interests above that of the commonwealth. Take the example of Representative Eddie Bernice Johnson, D-Texas.

The longtime congresswoman from Dallas is a member of the renowned Congressional Black Caucus. At 74, she is expected to easily win a 10th term in November over Republican Stephen Broden. Recently, Amy Goldson, counsel for the Congressional Black Caucus Foundation, said that Johnson violated organization rules when she awarded scholarships to her relatives and those of an aide, Rod Givens. Givens served as the district director for the people of the 30th Congressional District.

According to the Dallas Morning News, over the last five years, Johnson awarded up to $20,000 and a total of 15 scholarships to two grandsons, two great-nephews, and aide Rod Givens' children between 2005 and 2008. Each year, each member of the Black Caucus is given $10,000 to award scholarships. In 2009, Johnson selected 12 students to divide $10,000 from two scholarship programs; according to foundation records released Monday. Eight students got one scholarship. The four other students — the congresswoman's grandsons, Kirk and David Johnson, and her staffer's son and daughter, Julian and Mariyah Givens — got two apiece.

These scholarships were awarded in violation of Congressional Black Caucus Foundation eligibility rules, which require that winners live or study in the lawmaker's district as well as the anti-nepotism clause. Initially, Johnson denied violating the anti-nepotism regulation. Now she has changed her position, saying that she "unknowingly" broke Congressional Black Caucus Foundation rules. "While I am not ashamed of helping, I did not intentionally mean to violate any rules in the process," Johnson wrote in a statement released Aug. 30.

Johnson intimated that she might not have picked relatives had there been more qualified applicants. Johnson says she'll repay the scholarship funds by week's end. Johnson's actions are troubling since awarding the scholarships violated anti-nepotism rules and went to students who neither live nor study in her district.

### 80 - Friday, September 17, 2010

In theory, the Tea party is supposed to be a grass roots organization. It obtained its name from the historical time period in which the British Politician Charles Townshend, implemented some Acts for the colonies, in an effort to boost his political career (sounds familiar). This was the time after the Stamp Act. See the Original colonist objected to the Stamp Act saying it was an unneeded form of internal taxation. So Townshend decided to develop another tax that would be external that they could not possibly be against. As a result, the Townshend Act was passed in England, which imposed taxes on selected produced, that was imported to the colonies, one of which was Tea. Add to that a few years later the British Parliament also passed the Tea act which was designed to help the East India Company make some loot and form a monopoly on Tea around the world. To make a long story short, folk didn't like this, especially Samuel Adams and his Sons of Liberty. Now the rest is history.

If you did not know The Tea Party is all the rave this season. There is so much to go through that I will only name a few with brief bullet points and then make my comments.

Carl Paladino: This cat may take the cake. First he admits to sending or should I say forwarding emails with bestiality and racist jokes to his boys, for some strange reason I don't see being Muslim, Black or Hispanic. He is best known for the photo shopped images of President Obama and the First Lady "dressed" for a White House ball as a pimp and bottom bitch. Then there is a December 2008 email showing a video of African tribesmen performing a traditional dance. The video is entitled "Obama Inauguration Rehearsal." I could go on but just in case you want to you can find the emails here. And of Course, Paladino states for the record, he is not a racist. But what can you expect from a man who looks up to Grover Cleveland - a self-proclaimed, staunch racist and supporter of white supremacy.

Tom Tancredo: During the Tea Party National Convention, which was held in Nashville, Tennessee at the Gaylord Opryland Hotel, this former Colorado Congressmen took the lead talking about Immigrants and Obama – which seems to be the hip thing to do nowadays. He is remembered for asserting that many of the people who voted Obama into office "can't even spell the word vote or even speak English." He also spoke on what he called the "cult of multiculturalism" which is "aided by leftists." Lastly, he placed emphasis on letting the group know that "our culture is at stake" a culture "based on Judeo-Christian values whether people like it or not!" Tancredo also announced that he was going to be working with Roy Beck, executive director of Numbers USA (an anti-immigrant group with strong ties to white nationalists). In 2005, Tancredo suggested that that it would be OK to wipe the Muslim holy city of Mecca off the map in response to al-Qaeda.

Sonny Thomas: Thomas is the founder of the Springboro Tea Party. It is obvious that Twitter gave him more balls than he really had, when he tweeted "Illegal's everywhere today! So many spics makes me feel like a speck. Grrr. Where's my gun?" on March 21 of this year. Thomas is an uncontested candidate for a seat on the Warren County Republican Party's central committee in Ohio.

Now I don't really care about these folks. All I do know is that they seem to be both unknowledgeable of American History and civics and intolerant of others. They claim to be patriots and proponents of liberty but likely couldn't tell you about William Penn – the most tolerant patriot of the new world. The man for whom liberty and religious freedom: were lived and observed in his every word and action. But most Tea party folk wouldn't know about that. And don't take my word for it – ask Meghan McCain, daughter of John McCain. She said not all but a good portion display various forms of "innate racism."

I find these troubling times in America, and even reflective of a time when anything other than white was attacked, lynched and dismembered. The Tea Party may not be racist. I do know they hate being called racist but at the same time hate Muslims, Hispanics and black folk – heil Hitler. But don't trip, I just had a revelation, maybe Floyd Mayweather is a Tea Party Support - after all, he a racist too.

### 81 - Monday, September 20, 2010

The current climate in Washington is tense. Not only are the upcoming midterm elections expected to change the future political landscape, but so too will the recent rash of ethical complaints leveled at prominent Democrats.

Two longtime members of the Congressional Black Caucus, Charles Rangel, and Maxine Waters are being investigated for alleged ethics violations.

Both of the aforementioned have declined plea offers and have accepted to fight the charges publicly prior to the November elections.

Since the establishment of the Office of Congressional Ethics by Speaker of the House Nancy Pelosi in 2009, all eight individuals cited for alleged ethics violations have been members of the Congressional Black Caucus, meaning all are African American. As such, many are starting to question if these investigations are racially or politically motivated.

The recent allegations against Congressman Rangel, who faces 13 ethics charges, including improper fundraising and tax evasion, and Congresswoman Maxine Waters, whom the House ethics subcommittee has alleged broke ethics rules by lobbying Treasury officials for a $25 million bailout of One United Bank in Boston, have given Congress a witch hunt environment. Waters' husband, former NFL player Sidney Williams, has a financial stake in One United.

In addition, the GOP has incessantly promoted an all-out ground assault against President Obama. Ironically all of this is happening while Republicans are trying to make the upcoming elections a referendum against the Democrat-controlled Congress and White House.

If the trials of Rangel and Waters do manifest, they may serve the interests of the GOP by driving a wedge between the Democratic Party, mainly the Obama White House, and his large corpus of African American supporters, and white Democrats.

The strange thing is that what Rangel and Waters are charged with is historically no different than activities conducted by former President George W. Bush.

Although to the dismay of many Democrats, Obama refused to charge the Bush administration with any criminal acts regarding his war against Iraq and his involvement with Enron.

135

During the first nine months of his administration, Bush used his presidential powers to assist his personal friend, Enron CEO Kenneth Lay, in covering up criminal activity. Bush fought vehemently against imposing caps on the price of electricity in California when Enron drove up prices artificially by manipulating and controlling supply. In addition, under the Bush administration, Lay was able to influence the administration's energy policies. In fact, the chairman of the Federal Energy Regulatory Commission was replaced in 2001 after he started an investigation into the now-illegal complex derivative-financing schemes practiced by Enron.

However, the Republicans are willing to take the opposite road if they are able to win back the U.S. House of Representatives in November. Rep. Darrell Issa, R-Calif., has stated that he will launch several investigations of the Obama administration if he becomes chairman of the House Oversight and Government Reform Committee.

Of specific importance to Issa is the Obama administration's alleged interference in U.S. Senate races in Pennsylvania and Colorado. Issa has attacked the administration with ethical wrongdoing charges consistently since Obama took office.

The double standard with respect to how Republicans and Democrats are being treated in regards to ethics violations sends mixed messages to the African American community. First it looks as if the white Democratic leadership, in concert with the GOP, is targeting blacks singularly. Second, it lets the world see America's hypocrisy in regards to how Republicans are treated compared to black political officials, especially if one happens to be the first African-American president of the United States of America.

They say that America was founded upon many tenants, of which the escape from religious persecution in Europe was one. As a result, where we live today has become the most religiously diverse nation in the world. But insofar that this is the historic truth, the query remains, is such our strength or weakness?

I make this assertion as a form of observation rooted both in historic accuracy and human action. The latter in many respects being feculent and absurd, in particular if what people display reflects what they actually think and feel. Since it regards the practice of Islam in modern America.

Personally, modern day Islam, or really I should state Islamic fundamentalism is equal to or the same as the Christianity that was presented that found and established this nation. This is why I am confused by protesting against an Islamic community center in NYC near or around ground zero, or anywhere in America to the proposed burning of books by zealots. This to me reaffirms the selfish edict, that we alone are the chosen people of God – a lesson refuted via the practice of slavery and cemented via the blood of many before, and during the civil war.

The simple summary is that Islam is no more or less violent than Christianity. Just like some in Islam believe all outside of their belief are infidels, so was the view of the Spanish, who came to the new world, and forced with the Bible and threat of death the native Americans to accept Christianity (Catholicism) without question. But this lead to war and they eventually left New Mexico in 1680. This is one reason Pope Alexander VI in 1493, decreed that it was all right for Europeans to use non-whites in the name of God. Which was good for Bartolome de Las Casas, a Christian who came to the conclusion that African slaves were needed in Hispaniola after he had killed many of the indigenous people.

The lesson learned was that we couldn't use political machinery to force our beliefs on others. A lesson the puritans would learn, albeit in theory it is purported that they left Europe to save Christianity from the politics of the European Church. Which is another reason for them as now. I cannot discern any difference between Christianity during the founding of America for a group of people who saw themselves as the chosen people of God, or the fervor that arose out of the protestant reformation or evangelicals, or fundamentalist Islam and its predilection for Shari law.

Yes, the actions of John Winthrop are just like those of Osama Bin Laden. They both say the same thing: that if we are good by our God, that God will bless us. Just Like Billy Graham, for it was the Reverend Billy Graham and other white ministers who told Martin Luther King Jr. during the civil rights bus boycott that his actions were "not Christian and ungodly."

The aforementioned examples tell me that all, regardless of religious affiliation are off base – for intolerance and absolute conformity is never good or godly. Unfortunately, this is what defines both Islam and Christianity historically globally. Yes, the intolerance of Islam by American Christians and fundamentalist Muslims hatred of the West are the same. Just as slavery showed that whites perceived themselves selfishly as the chosen people of God, I see the same today. How the perspicacity of scripture is used to suggest how some selected few if differently is less than others. Unfortunately regardless of what men say, no God would assert such a premise. The bottom line is that truth fears no light and no man can love God yet ornate hate for his brother at the same time, for it is written that he that lives by the sword shall die by the sword, and both Christianity and Islam should take note.

## 83 - Monday, October 25, 2010

In January of this year, a 7.0-magnitude earthquake killed more than 250,000 people in Haiti. Since then the country has been struggling to rebuild and restore infrastructure. The response from the United States was immediate with USAID being charged by President Obama with leading the U.S. government's response to the crisis.

Ten months later many problems remain. More than a million Haitians are still living on the streets between piles of trash and rubble from destroyed buildings. Even more unfortunate is that none of the $1.15 billion the U.S. promised for rebuilding has arrived. Although 50 other nations pledged more than $8 billion for reconstruction, less than $700 million of that had reached Haiti as of the end of September. The money was pledged by Secretary of State Hillary Clinton and was to be used mostly for reconstruction.

One reason for the delay is that in the U.S., although both the House and the Senate passed a bill that would make $917 million available for aid to Haiti, the U.S. Senate has yet to pass an authorization bill that directs exactly how the money will be spent. This is because one senator, Tom Coburn, R-Okla., is holding up the bill because he is opposed to the creation of a senior Haiti coordinator because the United States currently has an ambassador to the country.

Meanwhile, deaths in Port-au-Prince are increasing due to a lack of food and shelter. Data shows a mere 2 percent of the debris and rubble from the earthquake have been removed and 13,000 temporary shelters have been built. A new report released by the international charity Oxfam indicates that the food aid pouring into Haiti is harming the country's economy, especially its agricultural sector. The majority of Haitians depend on agriculture for their livelihood but instead of AID we let disease fester - and we knew this would happen.

139

The only good thing is that stateside resident Wyclef did not run for president or it would have been worse. Remember a song by UGK back in the day that said "*movies got these boy's f\*\*\*\*d up in the minds.*" It specifically reminds me of celebrities and how some with fame think that's all they need to do anything, along with money and popularity that is.

Unless you have been under a rock, you should have heard by now that Wyclef Jean, the producer, singer and songwriter of the infamous Fugee's has indicated he plans to run for president of Haiti. Also, that the almost son-in-law of former vice presidential candidate Sarah Palin is also throwing his hat into the political ring and is running for mayor of his hometown, Wasilla, Alaska. Johnston's manager, Tank Jones, confirmed that Johnston's campaign is part of a reality TV show.

I do not know Palin, Johnston or Wyclef, but I will make a broad statement that none of the aforementioned are qualified to be Mayor or President. Why might you ask?

Unfortunately, money and fame may get you the attention and the votes to win an office, but it does not qualify one with the proficiencies in economics, health management or a knowledge in parliamentary procedures required to make a substantial contribution to a major governmental body. In addition, it requires a substantial knowledge base to discern, understand and solve the problems one is confronted with and discuss them with advisers and experts in their selected fields.

I think Wyclef Jean is not qualified to be president of Haiti for the same reasons I thought Palin was not qualified to be vice president of the U.S. His candidacy is a cover up for U.S. military occupation of the country. The truth is that Jean has extremely cozy relationships with Bill Clinton and others who desire via neo-colonialism to make Haiti a tourist location for the rich and a mass pool of cheap labor for U.S. commercial interest and factories.

Jean was the former Ambassador to the U.S. and his uncle currently serves in that post. While Ambassador, he never met with the United Nations, World bank, the IMF nor any other major international political body. If he wanted to make a difference he should run for a seat in New York or New Jersey, supporting the interest of the millions of urban Americans who made him rich, but he won't. Cause the way I see it he is either the black Sarah Palin or Levi Johnston - all letting the people of Haiti die regardless.

### 84 - Wednesday, November 03, 2010

Imagine this; Fred Sanford is at home, sitting down listening to the election returns from around the nation on his radio from NPR. Well not really, imagine me at home in the bed listening to the national election results on the radio, after all, that's what amounted for my entertainment last night. All I could say to myself, upon return upon return were Mr. Sanford's legendary description of his son Lamont "you big dummy."

It seemed to fit the evening correctly, both in terms of describing the democrats and the Obama administration and the fools who voted the GOP in the office around the country by a historic level. I may be wrong, but not since 1948, when Truman was president have we seen such a large takeover of the house by one party. We know what happened nationally, now in the US House of representatives, the GOP controls 239 seats, a pickup of 60 and also added 10 gubernatorial seats that they swiped from democrats

But even more, troubling is what occurred on the state levels. In Georgia for example, the second Republican governor was elected in a row since 2002. Prior to this Georgia had not had a Republican Governor since Reconstruction. And for your history buffs that is since Benjamin Conley in

141

1872, who ironically was one of the persons who assisted in promoting harsh resolutions condemning the state's failure to comply with the Reconstruction Acts of Congress in the organization of the General Assembly in an effort to re-seat the colored members, kicked out by democrats. "A former Whig, Conley had opposed secession and retired to his plantation near Montgomery, Alabama, for the duration of the war. On his return to Georgia after the surrender, it was natural for him to join the Republicans and to support the congressional plan for Reconstruction."

Anyhow, back to my point. In the state house the won 17 seats giving republicans 107 of the 180 seats and in the senate the control 37 of the 56 district senate seats.

Now, what caused this? I don't listen to pundits, but I have my own developed postulate on the outcome. Now unlike many I don't credit this to the Tea (Taxed enough Already) party, and don't understand how folk, especially black folk can suggest such when they likely don't even know what the acronym stand for or their beliefs, albeit most of which are rooted in agoraphobic based nativism. But I can say first and foremost is President Obama.

President Obama selfish tendencies and his ethnicity brought this on. Only a fool, taking office after George W. Bush, who inherited an economy in shambles and on the brink of collapse, would put health care before jobs and stabilization of the dollar. I just don't get it, I mean it seems to be misdirected attention to spending 18 of your first 23 months on passing health care with the way the market and unemployment situation is currently. Moreover, Obama also appointed some foxes (Geithner and Summers) to run the hen house and allowed them to suggest policy, without critical examination to solve the economic crisis that history tells us would not be able to improve the economy that has taken 20 years to get this bad in a two-year period.

All of this has made me prophetic since two years ago I stated that the "Obamafication of America" blinded people and we were moving from "Tobe to Joe Six-Pack." Now the lunatics run the asylum.

Now Obama has to depend on Black folks to keep him in office, since he may lose the Latino electorate given he promised to deal with comprehensive immigration reform in his first year – which he did not, just as he promised to address needle exchange – which he did not.

The tea party is another issue. It seems that they do not understand that one cannot fix an economy as bad as ours in one or two years (idiots). Plus they are dishonest, for if the pundits knew anything and were honest, they would call this election for what it was. No, this is not an anti-incumbent protest vote; it was an anti-democratic incumbent vote. No, it was not anti-Obama vote; it was an anti-Black man as president vote. Which in summary means that this vote was directed to punish democrats for promoting and getting a black man elected as President.

Black folk if we were smart could learn something from the tea party. Instead of voting democratic without question, and complain about the GOP, if they truly desired change they would join the GOP, and vote for their own kind and once elected form their own political coterie. But clear this clearly requires too much though and many, as I said drank the Kool-Aid – since they were just happy to have a black man as president. See what a vote does, nothing, for America is not a democracy it is a republic – and only land-owners make decisions in republics, You big dummy. Now we have a collection of Andrew Jackson's all over the place and all that is missing now is David Duke. Arizona just passed by a large margin, Prop 107, legislation that bans preferential treatment and discrimination prohibition (Affirmative Action) so the way I see it it's on and all downhill from here - thanks for nothing.

143

Since the Democratic party took an old-fashioned butt whipping from the GOP during the midterm elections, one can only assume that their "just say no" mantra and incessant attacks on President Obama and his administration will not only continue, but might even accelerate and become more pointed.

As a result, we should all be on guard for the Republican-dominated Congress, along with the assistance of Fox news and other right-wing extremist groups, to ask for investigations into the fledgling Obama administration. If this speculation is true, then there are several areas for certain that the GOP will likely target over the next few years.

First, based on what has already transpired over the past two years, it is clear that Representatives Darrell Issa, R-Calif., and Lamar Smith R-Texas, will likely lead the charge. Both have been attacking the Obama administration since day one through often strange and bizarre press releases. Now after this past Tuesday, they actually have some pull, since they will most probably become the chairs of the House Committee on Oversight and Government Reform and the House Judiciary Committee, respectively. And what does this mean; it means that they now have the power to subpoena presidential staff and appointees. But what will they investigate?

Well, based on all of the attention Attorney General Eric Holder received for not investigating the New Black Panther Party, one should expect to see a monumental government waste of money on this. The Obama administration decided to limit the scope of the civil case and the Department of Justice was strongly criticized by the GOP for dropping the case against some of the members of the party. Then there will also be some interest in how the administration dealt with the BP Gulf of Mexico oil spill. Issa has made it clear that he had some major issues with how the president handled the natural disaster, stating that the Obama administration was more concerned about his image than the oil spill.

Whatever happens, it will be very interesting. It won't be a surprise if they decide to hold hearings on his religious beliefs or whether he was truly born in America. So the question is, how long will it take for the Republican-led House to start investigating the Obama administration?

If they do, it will show me just how stupid the GOP and worse, how much they hate America. If they were competent and loved this great country, they would focus on the nation and not politics. It is as if they cannot see how China is running around us like the Roadrunner. China has the world's longest network of high-speed rail, giving China more high-speed rail tracks than the rest of the world put together. But Republicans don't see this and say stupid things like they do not want high-speed rail. That is what the Governors-elect of Wisconsin (Scott Walker) and Ohio (John Kasich) said during their campaigns. This has also been a point made by Rep. John Mica, R-Fla., and the committee's ranking GOP member, who said that he believes high-speed trains are a good idea, but doesn't agree with the projects selected by the Transportation Department for funding. Other idiots include New Jersey Governor Chris Christie and Florida, Governor-elect Rick Scott.

Republicans have shown they are the party of no, but now they are the party of China, doing all they can to make certain the pass us by as number one in the world as soon as they can.

## 86 - Thursday, December 23, 2010

A few years ago on an August day, a pact was made between the United States and Poland to deploy US-made 'interceptor missiles' on Polish soil. Although it was implemented under the penumbra of protecting European NATO allies from a

Russian nuclear attack - a move that some considered to be a dangerous move towards nuclear war.

The US also planned to deploy radar in the Czech Republic as part of this missile defense system and a US-controlled missile shield for Europe and North America. In theory, it is to protect western nations and us from so-called potential "rogue states," such as Iran but the real deal is Russia.

This is why START is so important for the Obama administration. A while back Russian President Vladimir Putin exposed the shallowness of the US propaganda line by offering a startled President Bush that Russia would offer the US use of Russian-leased radar facilities in Azerbaijan on the Iran border to far better monitor Iran missile launches. The Bush Administration simply ignored the offer, exposing that their real target is Russia. In addition, the signing of the agreement may lessen tensions between Russia and NATO and reduce the probability of a brand new Cold War arms race in theory.

Obama backs missile defense too but has canceled plans to station an anti-ballistic missile system in Poland and the Czech Republic. Obama's foreign policy adviser is Zbigniew Brzezinski and his foreign policy team in addition to father Zbigniew Brzezinski, includes Brzezinski's son, Ian Brzezinski, current US Deputy Assistant Secretary of Defense for European and NATO Affairs. Ian Brzezinski - all supporters of US missile defense policy.

It was just last year that Obama said he was not going to go with the Bush plans in Poland. But how quickly things change. Refusing to continue the Bush-era proposal is what maybe got the deal signed with Russia in the first place - a deal which was signed in April. What is for certain are the comments by Czech Prime minister Jan Fischer, who has indicated that Obama said the US was suspending efforts in Poland but did not give any specific reason.

146

How quickly do things change? Obama has flip-flopped - in order to get the START treaty signed, he has now agreed to continue with Bush's proposed US controlled missile shield in Europe. Less than two weeks ago President Barack Obama committed the United States to "basing land-based SM-3 interceptors in Poland in the 2018 timeframe as part of its NATO" - wide missile defense system in a joint statement with Polish President Bronislaw Komorowski when he came to the White House,

They said that detractors of the new START treaty disagree with the preamble of the treaty which contains the following statement, but it seems that Obama has had the last word, getting it passed and all he had to do was give the GOP what Bush desired - a missile defense system in Poland designed to keep an eye on Russia more so than North Korea and Iran.

Last I heard the United States was supposedly a bastion of democracy. You know freedom of expression, speech, information, and religion. But it seems that only is consistent and true when expression, speech and religion are in support of the United Sates.

I find it strange that the principles that we as a nation promote that make us different and stand out, that the rest of the world - namely democracy, and what we fight for in other places is really just a willy nilly catch phrase. It is OK for us to put and plant what we think and call democracy in places like Iraq and Afghanistan - even if folk do not want such or even if we fail. But when other folks use our idealistic tendencies it becomes sacrilegious.

Our "imperial arrogance" asserts I guess, that the only folks with rights to a free and open society on us and no one else. We have the audacity to proclaim being open, democratic and proponents of the free sharing of information unless it pertains to information of ours. Then we become the incarnate of Mussolini and fascism. The expression is obviously OK except for the Internet. Why? I cannot answer, but I can say we use our power to make private enterprises including PayPal and Amazon.com and master card to control what the supreme courts have considered expression as well - money when anything we disagree with is cited or revealed. It is just ridiculous, the greatest democracy in the world asking for an Internet site to be shut down and its owner killed or jailed for sharing information that he did not steal.

How quick we are to reference Thomas Jefferson but forget it was he who wrote, "Information is the currency of democracy." I just find it two-faced to say on the one hand we are a Nation of liberty and freedom yet on the other hold freedom of the Internet as being completely different. Even condemning China for their censorship but we espouse the same behavior and practice from a governmental location regarding WikiLeaks. Common sense tells me that if one condemns WikiLeaks we have to do the same with the New York Times and other websites.

Freedom in the US is a myth. This is the only postulate that can be contrived from this entire WikiLeaks fiasco. Such is even more convoluted when we have no laws to even assert criminal behavior on the websites owner's behalf outside of an outdated 1917 espionage act that deals with maps.

# ABOUT THE AUTHOR

Torrance Stephens is originally from Memphis, Tennessee. He attended Morehouse College where he studied, psychology, biology and chemistry. He received a master's degree in Educational Psychology and Measurement from Atlanta University and a Ph.D. in Counseling from Clark Atlanta University. He has lived in Nigeria, Senegal, South Africa and several other African countries working with Africare International and conducting Infectious disease research. He is the author of several books including a novel, poems, essays and several collections of short prose. He was an Assistant Professor at Emory University in the Rollins School of Public Health in Atlanta for more than 14 years and until recently, as Associate Professor and Health Education/Health Promotion Track Coordinator for the MPH program at Morehouse School of Medicine in the Department of Community and Preventive Medicine. He is the father of two and currently lives in Palmetto, Georgia, and teaches Statistics and Neurology and Behavior at Clark Atlanta University in the Departments of Psychology and School of Education.

www.ingramcontent.com/pod-product-compliance
Lightning Source LLC
Chambersburg PA
CBHW072126280526
45788CB00002B/570